THE GREATEST PRAYER

Also by John Dominic Crossan

Nonfiction
The Historical Jesus
Jesus: A Revolutionary Biography
Who Killed Jesus?
The Birth of Christianity
A Long Way from Tipperary
Excavating Jesus (with Jonathan L. Reed)
In Search of Paul (with Jonathan L. Reed)
The Last Week (with Marcus J. Borg)
The First Christmas (with Marcus J. Borg)
God and Empire
The First Paul (with Marcus J. Borg)

The Greatest Prayer

REDISCOVERING THE REVOLUTIONARY

MESSAGE OF THE LORD'S PRAYER

John Dominic Crossan

HarperOne
An Imprint of HarperCollinsPublishers

HarperOne

All biblical quotations are taken from the New Revised Standard Version or are the author's own translation, unless otherwise noted.

THE GREATEST PRAYER: *Rediscovering the Revolutionary Message of the Lord's Prayer.* Copyright © 2010 by John Dominic Crossan. All rights reserved. Printed in the United States of America. No part of this book may be used or reproduced in any manner whatsoever without written permission except in the case of brief quotations embodied in critical articles and reviews. For information, address HarperCollins Publishers, 195 Broadway, New York, NY 10007.

HarperCollins books may be purchased for educational, business, or sales promotional use. For information, please e-mail the Special Markets Department at SPsales@harpercollins.com.

HarperCollins website: http://www.harpercollins.com

HarperCollins®, 📖®, and HarperOne™ are trademarks of HarperCollins Publishers

FIRST HARPERCOLLINS PAPERBACK EDITION PUBLISHED IN 2011
Designed by Level C

Library of Congress Cataloging-in-Publication Data

Crossan, John Dominic.
The greatest prayer : rediscovering the revolutionary message of the lord's prayer / John Dominic Crossan.
p. cm.
ISBN 978-0-06-187568-7
1. Lord's prayer—Meditations. I. Title.
BV230.C77   2011
242'.722—dc22   2010007898

HB 01.19.2023

For
Canon Marianne Wells Borg
and
The Center for Spiritual Development
of
Trinity Episcopal Cathedral, Portland, Oregon

Contents

The Strangest Prayer

The Lord's Prayer is Christianity's greatest prayer. It is also Christianity's strangest prayer. It is prayed by all Christians, but it never mentions Christ. It is prayed in all churches, but it never mentions church. It is prayed on all Sundays, but it never mentions Sunday. It is called the "Lord's Prayer," but it never mentions "Lord."

It is prayed by fundamentalist Christians, but it never mentions the inspired inerrancy of the Bible, the virgin birth, the miracles, the atoning death, or bodily resurrection of Christ. It is prayed by evangelical Christians, but it never mentions the *evangelium,* or gospel. It is prayed by Pentecostal Christians, but it never mentions ecstasy or the Holy Spirit.

It is prayed by Congregational, Presbyterian, Episcopalian, and Roman Catholic Christians, but it never mentions congregation, priest, bishop, or pope. It is prayed by Christians who split from one another over this or that doctrine, but it never mentions a single one of those doctrines. It is prayed by Christians who focus on Christ's substitutionary sacrificial atonement for human sin, but it never mentions Christ, substitution, sacrifice, atonement, or sin.

It is prayed by Christians who focus on the next life in heaven or in hell, but it never mentions the next life, heaven, or hell. It is prayed by Christians who emphasize what it never mentions and also prayed by Christians who ignore what it does.

You could respond, of course, that there is nothing strange there at all. It is, you might say, a Jewish prayer from the Jewish Jesus; hence nothing Christian or even Jewish Christian is present. But that only invites us to start the question of strangeness all over again. It does not mention covenant or law, Temple or Torah, circumcision or purity, and so on.

What if the Lord's Prayer is neither a Jewish prayer for Jews nor yet a Christian prayer for Christians? What if it is—as this book suggests—a prayer from the heart of Judaism on the lips of Christianity for the conscience of the world? What if it is—as this book suggests—a radical manifesto and a hymn of hope for all humanity in language addressed to all the earth?

———

The Lord's Prayer is, for me, both a revolutionary manifesto and a hymn of hope. It is *revolutionary,* because it presumes and proclaims the radical vision of *justice* that is the core of Israel's biblical tradition. It is a *hymn,* because it presumes and produces poetic techniques that are the core of Israel's biblical poetry.

In ordinary everyday language the word "justice" has come primarily, if not exclusively, to mean retributive justice, that is, punishment. For example, I was working on this Prologue while in Denver on September 27, 2009. The *Denver Post*'s Sunday headline was about "DUI Justice," and it discussed whether punishments were fairly and equally imposed on all accused persons. That headline took for granted that most readers would see the word "justice" and correctly understand that it meant punishment—judicial punishment, but punishment nonetheless.

But the primary meaning of "justice" is not *retributive,* but *distributive.* To be just means to distribute everything fairly. The primary meaning of "justice" is equitable distribution of *whatever* you have in mind—even if that is retribution or punishment.

Do not think this is some game with words. Here is what is at stake. The biblical tradition speaks of God as a God of "justice and righteousness" (Ps. 99:4; Isa. 33:5; Jer. 9:24). Those two words express the same content. A God of "justice and righteousness" is a God who does what is just by doing what is right and does what is right by doing what is just.

The redundant phrase proclaims that God's world must be distributed fairly and equitably among all God's people. Whenever, then, I use the term "justice" with respect to the biblical tradition, Jesus, or the Lord's Prayer, it will be distributive justice I have almost exclusively in mind.

When the biblical tradition proclaims that revolutionary vision of distributive justice, it is imagining neither liberal democratic principles nor universal human rights. Instead, its vision derives from the common experience of a well-run home, household, or family farm. If you walked into one, how would you judge the householder? Are the fields well tended? Are the animals properly provisioned? Are the buildings adequately maintained? Are the children and dependents well fed, clothed, and sheltered? Are the sick given special care? Are responsibilities and returns apportioned fairly? Do all have enough? Especially that: Do all have enough? Or, to the contrary, do some have far too little while others have far too much?

It is that vision of the well-run household, of the home fairly, equitably, and justly administered, that the biblical tradition applies to God. God is the Householder of the world house, and all those preceding questions must be repeated on a global and cosmic scale. Do all God's children have enough? If not—and the biblical answer is "not"—how must things change here below so that all God's people have a fair, equitable, and just proportion of God's world? The Lord's Prayer proclaims that necessary change as both revolutionary manifesto and hymn of hope.

Do not, by the way, let anyone tell you that is Liberalism, Socialism, or Communism. It is—if you need an -ism—Godism, Householdism or, best of all, Enoughism. We sometimes name that biblical vision of God's World-Household as Egalitarianism but, actually, Enoughism would be a more accurate description.

———

The Lord's Prayer is, to repeat, both a revolutionary manifesto and a hymn of radical hope. *Hope* is already included in calling the manifesto revolutionary—has there ever been a revolution that was not hopeful? But why call it a *hymn*—that is, a poem—of hope? It is certainly a prayer, but how is it a poetic prayer? And does that format matter?

Just as the *content* of the Lord's Prayer is deeply embedded in the biblical tradition of justice, so is its *format* deeply embedded in the biblical tradition of poetry. Both biblical justice and biblical poetry are recurring emphases in the Lord's Prayer.

Biblical poetry—whether it is in prophecy, psalm, or proverb—works especially with one major technique. That device is a parallelism in which the second part of a two-part sequence says more or less the same as the preceding one. But everything depends on that "more or less" factor.

The Bible's poetic parallelism is not simply a lazy redundancy in which the second part repeats the former one to give the oral poet time to think about what comes next. What happens is that the parallelism creates a vibration of thought, a metronome in the mind. It is a tick-tock effect that makes one wonder: Is exactly the same thing being said twice, or does the second part somehow expand on the first? And, if so, how?

In some examples of what is called *synonymous* parallelism, the redundancy seems to be quite complete. Here is a possible example from Psalm 8:4:

What are	human beings	that	you are mindful of	them,
	mortals	that	you care for	them?

But are those two lines totally redundant, or is there something new in that second line? Does God's "care for" us somehow specify or amplify that God is "mindful of" us? It makes you pause to think, does it not?

Here is another example, from Psalm 114:1:

When	Israel	went out	from	Egypt,
	the house of Jacob		from	a people of strange language,

"The house of Jacob" and "Israel" certainly mean the same people. But "house of Jacob" also recalls the whole saga of Joseph, which starts in Genesis 37. It reminds us that he was sold into Egyptian slavery by his brothers and eventually saved them all from starvation. It reminds us how "Israel" ended up in "Egypt" in the first place. It reminds us that "all the persons of the house of Jacob who came into Egypt were seventy" (46:27). That is not redundant with, but expansive of, the first line.

Poetic parallelism is a lure for meditation. Could it be, then, that the two halves of the Lord's Prayer—Matthew 6:9–10, which talks about the Father's name, kingdom, and will, and Matthew 6:11–13, which mentions bread, debts, and temptation—are in deliberate parallelism with each other? Poetic parallelism provokes thought, so I think a lot about that possibility and what it might mean.

Furthermore, that mental dialectic between parallel lines—that question of how much redundancy there is—is even more emphasized in synonymous parallelism when one line is in the negative ("not") and the other in the positive ("but"). Here is an example of that type of parallelism at the end of the Lord's Prayer in Matthew 6:13:

And	do not bring	us	to the time of trial,
but	rescue	us	from the evil one.

Poetic lines like that are often called *antithetical* parallelism, but the process still pushes the ear to hear and the mind to think whether they are exactly the same or whether the second line expands the content. Poetic parallelism is not just about aesthetics, but about interpretation.

Finally, the most fascinating type of parallelism in the Bible is called *stepped, climactic,* or *crescendo* parallelism. In that device, the lines are quite parallel in format, but the content increases toward a climax. Here is an example from Habakkuk 3:17:

Though	the fig tree	does not blossom,
and	no fruit	is on the vines;
Though	the produce of the olive	fails
and	the fields	yield no food;
Though	the flock	is cut off from the fold,
and	there is no herd	in the stalls,

Internally, each of those three examples of "though . . . and" shows a balanced parallelism: (1) fig and fruit, (2) olive and field, and (3) flock and herd. But, overall and externally, there is a crescendo from figs and vines through olives and cereals and on to flocks and herds. We will have to see, for example, whether this also applies to God's name, kingdom, and will in the first half of the Lord's Prayer and to our bread, debt, and temptation in its second half.

If any or all of that sounds too terribly technical, here is one famous example from a speech you probably know already, but whose roots in the Bible's poetic parallelism you may not have recognized. Friday, January 20, 1961, was a freezing winter's day in Washington, D.C., as John Fitzgerald Kennedy gave his inaugural address as the thirty-fifth president of the United States. In the climax at the end of his speech were two examples of poetic parallelism. Here is the first one:

And so, my fellow Americans:
ask not what your country can do for you—
ask what you can do for your country.

As we saw above, that balance of the negative "ask not" and the positive "ask" is called antithetical parallelism in the tradition of biblical poetry. It is also termed *reversed* parallelism, from the sequence "your country . . . you" and "you . . . your country."

Then, in the very next sentence President Kennedy gave another—but quite different—example of poetic parallelism:

My fellow citizens of the world:
ask not what America will do for you,
but what together we can do for the freedom of man.

You will notice immediately that President Kennedy did not follow the previous format and suggest the world should "ask not what America will do for you, but what you will do for America." Instead, he moved up a level from service for "America" to "freedom" for all the world. This is another example of stepped, climactic, or crescendo parallelism. In it the latter part moves beyond the former one in content despite similarity in format.

I will argue that, as the Lord's Prayer moves from God's "name" through "kingdom" to "will" in the first part and from "bread" through "debts" to "temptation" in the second part, there is a synonymous parallelism not only between those two parts, but even a crescendo parallelism within each part.

———

I conclude with a few comments on why and how I wrote this book. I have been thinking about Jesus in his first-century Jewish and Roman matrix for about forty years. One obvious way to test my conclusions about him was to see how they compared with the Lord's Prayer itself. I started with the presupposition that I would find in that prayer what the historical Jesus stood for—or knelt for. The *why* of writing, therefore, was to test my general understanding of Jesus against the specific details of his own ultimate prayer. I also chose to focus on Matthew's version as it is the best known and most used.

The *how* was both more complicated and more simple. An intuitive insight mentioned above was that the prayer came from Judaism and was transmitted through Christianity, but was ultimately for everyone. In other words, the entire biblical tradition flowed through every unit of this prayer. How was I to imagine the way in which Jesus, his first companions, or those first Christian Jews saw that biblical tradition? I certainly did not imagine they could read that entire magnificent tradition or had ever heard it all read orally to them.

What I did was to focus on the key words of the prayer: first, "Father," "name," "kingdom," "will," and then "bread," "debt," and "temptation." I simply ran each word through a computerized concordance of the Christian Bible, printed each result, and read those lists—in context—over and over again. As I read them, I thought about them until the dominant emphases of each word became more and more obvious. I then discussed each key word in the prayer within those wider biblical emphases. In other words, this book is a biblical meditation on the Lord's Prayer.

Finally, a word about my title, *The Greatest Prayer*. It is intended, first of all, within Christianity itself. It is surely our greatest prayer—whether we call it the "*Abba* Prayer" with the early Christians, the "Our Father" with the Catholic community, or the "Lord's Prayer" with Protestant tradition. It is certainly the official prayer of Christianity.

But I also intended that title as a challenge to religions other than Christianity. I have absolutely no presumption that the greatest prayer of Christianity must be, or even should be, the greatest prayer for other religions. But I ask this of any and all of them. Does your own greatest prayer speak exclusively to the followers of your religion? Or does it speak to the conscience of the entire world? I propose that the greatest prayer in every religion should speak to all the world and for all the earth.

1

Pray Then in This Way

We do not know how to pray as we ought.

Romans 8:26

There is a design team for airports whose special job is the location of public electricity outlets in passenger terminals. Their job is to make them as few, as inaccessible, and as invisible as is humanly possible. They are immensely talented and superbly successful at that assignment.

Over the last twenty years I have been in the air about every week to lecture at different churches in Canada and the United States. And every week I roam airport gates—or even airport lounges—in search of those elusive outlets as I wait for planes that are on time, late, or cancelled. I even carry a three-way plug so I can share with others whose outlet search has already been successful. I need electricity to charge my computer, which is, by the way, an Apple Macintosh, which I chose initially because the Bible proclaims that "those who look through the windows see dimly" (Eccl. 12:3).

In traveling, therefore, I think a lot about electricity, about how to find it and connect with it. I think about how incredibly powerful my MacBook Pro is, and yet how absolutely dependent it is on getting its battery regularly charged. And, in that process, I have found my metaphor, my generative, constitutive mega-metaphor, for prayer. In that metaphor we are all laptops, and prayer is about empowerment by participation in and collaboration with God.

Think about electricity as a metaphor or symbol for God. Do not respond that electricity is *only* a metaphor or *just* a symbol, because the alternative for the mystery of an invisible God is always some other metaphor or some different symbol. But tread carefully here, because metaphors create dreams and symbols create visions.

This God-as-Electricity is always there, whether discovered or not. Even when found, my human freedom allows me to connect or not connect. It never forces itself upon me. I need it without its needing me.

Furthermore, God-as-Electricity is equally available to all comers. You do not have to merit it by your action or deserve it by your character. You can be rich or poor, young or old, gay or straight, female or male, or anything else you can imagine.

Finally, God-as-Electricity works just as well for game and movie players, cell phones, and digital assistants; it even works equally well for Apples and PCs. All we laptops have to do is find an outlet and plug ourselves in; empowerment is the free gift of God-as-Electricity.

———

I imagine God-as-Electricity and think of prayer as empowerment by participation in and collaboration with God. But is that what the Christian Bible understands by God and by prayer? After all, the types and themes of the biblical book of Psalms fall into two major categories, and neither seems to emphasize participation or empowerment.

Psalms of Request. The first and largest category of the biblical psalms is psalms of *request*—made either indirectly through complaint and lament or directly through plea and petition. Those subcategories are, of course, very closely intertwined. Here are some examples of complaint or lament for either individual or community:

You have made your people suffer hard things;
    you have given us wine to drink that made us reel. (60:3)

Hear my voice, O God, in my complaint;
preserve my life from the dread enemy. (64:1)

I pour out my complaint before him;
I tell my trouble before him. (142:2)

The point of those prayers is not just to vent, whine, or emote, but to implore divine assistance by laying out the desperate situation of the individual or the community. And, furthermore, by asserting that it is God who has brought about that very situation, there is a quite obvious request for improved relations. Still, the emphasis is one of absolute trust—simply describing the difficulties is enough to ensure God's help and protection.

Besides that implicit or indirect mode of request, the biblical psalms contain numerous examples of explicit or direct request by plea and petition. Focus, for example, on words like "grant me/us" or "give me/us" in these psalms:

O grant us help against the foe,
for human help is worthless. (60:11; 108:12)

Show us your steadfast love, O Lord,
and grant us your salvation. (85:7)

Give me understanding . . . (119:34, 73, 125, 144, 169)

Give me life . . . (119:37, 40, 107, 154, 156)

Psalm 119 repeats like a drumbeat its requests for understanding and life five times each. In those examples you have, once again, that oscillation between the individual and the communal request for assistance and deliverance.

Some of those prayers of request are positive (for us) and some are negative (against them); some are for an individual and some are for the community; some are implicit, by complaint or lament, and some are explicit, by plea or petition. But in one form or another *request* is the dominant type of biblical prayer. It is important to notice that, as in the final example, even a personal request does not mean self-centered individualism, but a plea for union with God, for "understanding, that I may keep your law and observe it with my whole heart" (119:34) and for "life according to your justice" (119:156).

Psalms of Gratitude. In the magnificent biblical book of Psalms the second largest category is psalms of *gratitude*. Sometimes the key word is "praise," but at other times it is "give thanks." Very often, however, those two terms appear in poetic parallelism; "praise" in one half verse is balanced by "thanksgiving" in the corresponding half verse:

> Sing praises to the Lord, O you his faithful ones,
>   and give thanks to his holy name. (30:4)

> We . . . will give thanks to you forever;
>   from generation to generation we will recount your praise.
>   (79:13)

> I will give thanks to you, O Lord, among the peoples,
>   and I will sing praises to you among the nations. (108:3)

The rhythm of prayer in the biblical book of Psalms is that double chant of request followed by gratitude, petition by thanksgiving, and complaint by praise. Whether we look at general types through the entire book of Psalms or themes within individual psalms, that is the dyad that appears again and again.

It is also, of course, a sequence we know full well from the ordinary and everyday human experience of appealing for something and then acknowledging its donor. "Please" and "Thanks" are likewise the systolic and diastolic beats of the Psalter's biblical heart. But that very dynamism of request and gratitude raises some very fundamental questions about the purpose of prayer.

Is prayer primarily or even exclusively about our wants and needs— even our most altruistic and other-focused ones? Is the combination of request and gratitude primarily or even exclusively about keeping an open contact with divine assistance that both thanks God for past positive responses and ensures future ones? Is Christian prayer a careful cost accounting that thanks God for what has already come our way and praises God for what is yet to follow it? Bluntly, succinctly, is prayer all about me, you, us, and a God who must be regularly praised and complimented for favors past, present, and yet to come?

Based on those biblical psalms, our Christian prayer is full of *request of God* through complaint and petition. It is likewise full of *gratitude to God* through praise and thanksgiving. But does Christian prayer also involve *empowerment by God* through participation and collaboration? I turn next, as a first step toward answering that question, from the biblical psalms to the biblical prophets. I move from those who spoke *to* God to those who spoke *for* God.

———

Something surprising happens, however, when you turn from the biblical psalms to the biblical prophets. Something strange happens when you compare those who speak *to* God in prayer with those who speak *for* God in prophecy. It is almost as if prophecy and prayer are at war with each other. But how can that be true?

Firmly grounded in the divine dream of Israel's Torah, the Bible's prophetic vision insists that God demands the fair and equitable sharing of God's world among all of God's people. In Israel's Torah, God says, "The land is mine; with me you are but aliens and tenants" (Lev. 25:23). We are all tenant farmers and resident aliens in a land and on an earth not our own.

The prophets speak in continuity with that radical vision of the earth's divine ownership. They repeatedly proclaim it with two words in poetic parallelism. "The Lord is exalted," proclaims Isaiah. "He dwells on high; he filled Zion with *justice and righteousness*" (33:5). "I am the Lord," announces Jeremiah in the name of God. "I act with steadfast love, *justice, and righteousness* in the earth, for in these things I delight" (9:24). And those qualities must flow from God to us, from heaven to earth. "Thus says the Lord," continues Jeremiah. "Act with *justice and righteousness,* and deliver from the hand of the oppressor anyone who has been robbed. And do no wrong or violence to the alien, the orphan, and the widow, or shed innocent blood in this place" (22:3).

"Justice and righteousness" is how the Bible, as if in a slogan, summarizes the character and spirit of God the Creator and, therefore, the destiny and future of God's created earth. It points to *distributive* justice as the Bible's radical vision of God. "Ah, you who join house to house, who add field to field," mourns the prophet Isaiah, "until there is room for no one but you, and you are left to live alone in the midst of the land" (5:8). But that landgrab is against the dream of God and the hope of Israel. Covenant with a God of distributive justice who owns the earth necessarily involves, the prophets insist, the exercise of distributive justice in God's world and on God's earth. All God's people must receive a fair share of God's earth.

The prophetic insistence that those in covenant with a God of justice and righteousness must also live in justice and righteousness is clear enough. But what do the prophets say about prayer—in all its aspects, from simple words of request and gratitude to more formal acts of ritual and sacrifice? This is where something strange occurs. They do not insist—as we might expect—that God demands *both* prayer *and* justice. They do not say we must *both* pray with fervor *and* act with justice.

Instead, they insist that God *does not want* prayer, ritual, liturgy, or sacrifice, *but wants instead* that righteous justice rule not only the land of Israel, but all the earth. Why put it that way? Why that negative opposition—against prayer—rather than a simple and serene assertion of the positive—for justice? Why do the prophets repeatedly set up a clash that creates a chasm between prayer and justice? And does that help or hinder this book on the Lord's Prayer? I look first at the evidence.

That rejection of ritual prayer in favor of distributive justice appears in prophets from Amos, Hosea, First Isaiah, and Micah in the 700s BCE, through Jeremiah in the late 600s BCE, to Third Isaiah in the late 500s BCE. (There are, by the way, three chronologically successive sections in the book of Isaiah: First Isaiah, chapters 1–39, from the later eighth century BCE; Second Isaiah, chapters 40–55, from the earlier sixth century BCE; and Third Isaiah, chapters 56–66, from the later sixth century BCE.)

I emphasize those dates for Israel's prophets because they were turbulent and even terrible years both at home and abroad. On the international level, in the period 911 to 539 BCE, the Assyrian Empire came to power and then fell before the Babylonian Empire, which rose and then in turn succumbed to the Persian Empire. On the local level, during those imperial transitions, first, the northern half of the Jewish homeland, known as the Kingdom of Israel, was destroyed by the Assyrians. Next, the southern half, known as the Kingdom of Judah, was destroyed by the Babylonians and its entire leadership taken into exile in Babylon; later, under Persian control, the exiles were allowed to return.

Throughout those seismic disturbances, that prophetic challenge of distributive justice rather than ritual prayer remained constant and consistent. In what follows, therefore, watch how the negative usually precedes and even overshadows the positive. And wonder to yourself why they speak that way. Why is justice set against prayer rather than joined together with it?

The 700s BCE. I begin with the prophet Amos, from the first half of that eighth century BCE. He was shocked to the soles of his peasant sandals by the ever growing inequality between rich and poor during the long rule of Jeroboam II over the Kingdom of Israel in the northern half of the Jewish homeland. His metaphors are brutal and shocking and must have seared at least the ears if not the hearts of his aristocratic hearers. But I focus here, in this first statement, on the striking dichotomy between prayer and justice. God is speaking through the prophet:

Negative: I hate, I despise your festivals, and I take no delight in your solemn assemblies. Even though you offer me your burnt offerings and grain offerings, I will not accept them; and the offerings of well-being of your fatted animals I will not look upon. Take away from me the noise of your songs; I will not listen to the melody of your harps.

Positive: But let justice roll down like waters, and righteousness like an ever-flowing stream. (5:21–24)

Once again, by the way, we find that parallelism between "justice" and "righteousness." It reminds us that both terms mean distributive justice in the biblical tradition.

Next, I turn to the prophet Hosea, in the second half of that same eighth century BCE, and we are still in that northern Kingdom of Israel. Assyrian incursions are gathering force, and the small kingdoms of Israel and Syria are seeking alliances with others against Assyria's military might. But once again, God is speaking through the prophet with the same disjunction between worship and justice:

For I desire steadfast love [*positive*] and not sacrifice [*negative*],
    the knowledge of God [*positive*] rather than burnt offerings
    [*negative*]. (6:6)

It is the same message that Amos gave us, but now reduced to two terse sentences in an even poetic parallelism of positive and negative: love and knowledge of God over and against sacrifice and offerings to God.

Then, still in the second half of that eighth century, but now in the southern Kingdom of Judah, that same indictment appears at the very start of First Isaiah:

Negative: What to me is the multitude of your sacrifices? says the Lord; I have had enough of burnt offerings of rams and the fat of fed beasts; I do not delight in the blood of bulls, or of lambs, or of goats. When you come to appear before me, who

asked this from your hand? Trample my courts no more; bringing offerings is futile; incense is an abomination to me. New
moon and sabbath and calling of convocation—I cannot endure
solemn assemblies with iniquity. Your new moons and your appointed festivals my soul hates; they have become a burden to
me, I am weary of bearing them. When you stretch out your
hands, I will hide my eyes from you; even though you make
many prayers, I will not listen; your hands are full of blood.

Positive: Wash yourselves; make yourselves clean; remove the evil
of your doings from before my eyes; cease to do evil, learn to do
good; seek justice, rescue the oppressed, defend the orphan,
plead for the widow. (1:11–17)

In the biblical tradition the prophetic God demands distributive
justice especially for those socially, structurally, and systemically
vulnerable: widows and orphans, who lack husbands and fathers in a
patriarchal society, and resident aliens, who lack familial protection in
a tribal society.

Furthermore, still in the last half of that internationally volatile
eighth century and still in the southern Kingdom of Judah, the
prophet Micah gives that same message more gently, as a human
question rather than a divine indictment:

Negative: With what shall I come before the Lord, and bow
myself before God on high? Shall I come before him with burnt
offerings, with calves a year old? Will the Lord be pleased with
thousands of rams, with ten thousands of rivers of oil? Shall I
give my firstborn for my transgression, the fruit of my body for
the sin of my soul?

Positive: He has told you, O mortal, what is good; and what does
the Lord require of you but to do justice, and to love kindness,
and to walk humbly with your God? (6:6–8)

The northern Kingdom of Israel did not survive the 700s BCE, but for the southern Kingdom of Judah the 600s and 500s moved from catastrophe to euphoria. Still, that prophetic demand for distributive justice *against* ritual prayer continued.

The 600s BCE. The fullest exposition of that disjunction between prayer and justice appears in the prophet Jeremiah soon after the Assyrian Empire succumbed to the Babylonian Empire at the end of the 600s BCE.

Jeremiah is commanded by God to stand before the gates of Jerusalem's Temple and address the worshipers who enter there to pray. They are not to think that prayer alone is enough, that the Temple is like a den, a hideaway, a safe house for those who have robbed and despoiled the poor. "Do not trust," God says, "in these deceptive words: 'This is the temple of the Lord, the temple of the Lord, the temple of the Lord.'. . . Has this house, which is called by my name, become a den of robbers in your sight?" (7:4, 11). Notice, then, the repeated "ifs" italicized in this warning:

> For *if* you truly amend your ways and your doings, *if* you truly act justly one with another, *if* you do not oppress the alien, the orphan, and the widow, or shed innocent blood in this place, and *if* you do not go after other gods to your own hurt, then I will dwell with you in this place, in the land that I gave of old to your ancestors forever and ever. (7:5–7)

On the other hand, *if* they continue to substitute worship for justice, God threatens to destroy the Temple itself, so that they will be unable to do so any longer.

That divine threat, by the way, almost cost Jeremiah his life: "The priests and the prophets and all the people laid hold of him, saying, 'You shall die!'" (26:8). But, eventually, "the officials and all the people said to the priests and the prophets, 'This man does not deserve the sentence of death, for he has spoken to us in the name of the Lord our God'" (26:16).

The 500s BCE. Finally, the Assyrian and Babylonian Empires were gone, and the Persian Empire had arrived; the northern Kingdom of Israel was gone forever, and the southern Kingdom of Judah had been restored after the Babylonian exile. It was the end of the 500s, but the unknown prophet we now call Third Isaiah had exactly that same ancient message about prayer and worship versus justice and righteousness. But now at least the positive predominates over the negative:

Negative: Is such the fast that I choose, a day to humble oneself? Is it to bow down the head like a bulrush, and to lie in sackcloth and ashes? Will you call this a fast, a day acceptable to the Lord?

Positive: Is not this the fast that I choose: to loose the bonds of injustice, to undo the thongs of the yoke, to let the oppressed go free, and to break every yoke? Is it not to share your bread with the hungry, and bring the homeless poor into your house; when you see the naked, to cover them, and not to hide yourself from your own kin? (58:5–7)

Throughout almost three centuries the God of the prophets demands distributive justice on this earth. That we have always known. But this is my seminal question: Why does the prophetic God insist on that negative and positive dynamic? Why insist—and insist so strongly—that God *does not want* prayer, ritual, worship, and sacrifice, *but rather wants* distributive justice, so that all God's people—and especially its most vulnerable members—get enough, get a fair share of God's world?

Here are some different ways of explaining why the prophets put it that way. One interpretation takes it to mean that we should stop wasting our time with prayer or worship and concentrate instead on justice and equality. Another understanding takes it as simply extremist language emphasizing that God wants *both* prayer *and* justice, not one or the other but both together. A final reading takes it as asserting that God prefers justice over prayer. The prophets were simply using shock tactics to emphasize God's preferential option for justice over prayer. After all, although God often speaks of rejecting prayer in the absence of justice, God never speaks of rejecting justice in the absence of prayer.

I wonder, however, if any of those is an adequate explanation for the interaction of prayer and justice in the biblical tradition. Is there a better way of holding together the biblical prophets on justice and the biblical psalms on prayer? After all, one of those very psalms also hails God as "Mighty King, lover of justice," saying, "You have established equity; you have executed *justice and righteousness* in Jacob" (99:4).

My own interpretation places those prophetic assertions of justice *against* prayer back into a dynamic and organic unity of justice-and-prayer or prayer-and-justice. In my understanding, meditation *and* action or ritual prayer *and* distributive justice can be distinguished, but not separated. They are like two sides of a coin that exist only as a unity. On a coin you can certainly *distinguish* heads from tails, but you cannot *separate* them and still have a coin. Even a preference for one side over the other cannot create separation.

Interpreting those prophetic claims as hyperbolic shock language tends to separate prayer from justice—even in terms of divine preference. But my proposal is that, although those two aspects of biblical religion can be distinguished, they cannot be separated. The twin sides of a coin, I repeat, cannot be separated without both sides being destroyed. You may prefer heads to tails or tails to heads, but if you attempt to have only one of them, you will end up with neither. On the one hand, since God is a God of justice, you cannot pray to such a God in a state of injustice—not, at least, without insincerity or even hypocrisy. On the other, to pray sincerely and with integrity to such a God risks empowerment by that God for that same justice.

Recall my initial "parable of the elusive outlet" and my metaphor of God-as-Electricity. You can certainly *distinguish,* but you cannot *separate* plugging in and charging up your laptop's battery. Imagine a silly argument about which was more important, which you should prefer, or whether you could do one without the other. One says, "Plugging in is more important." Another says, "No, charging up is more important." We know that those two operations are reciprocal and dialectical, that each presumes the other, and, that, although we are free not to plug in, we are not free, thereafter, to avoid charging up. If, in other words, you have prayer without justice or justice without prayer, my understanding is that you have neither—no justice, and no prayer either.

To confirm—but also deepen—my proposal of the interactive relationship between justice and prayer, I turn from the Old Testament to the New Testament in the Christian Bible. I turn to Paul and his interpretation of the Lord's Prayer. Perhaps you are thinking, wait a moment, there is no version of the Lord's Prayer anywhere in Paul's letters. But would Paul himself agree with that judgment?

We know the "Our Father" or the Lord's Prayer in several original versions. In this book I focus on Matthew 6:9–13, because it is the best-known and most-used version. But there is also a somewhat different one in Luke 11:2–4. And, apart from those two texts in the New Testament, there is also one outside it. This is in a first-century manual of church practice known as *The Teaching* (*Didachē* in Greek; see the Appendix).

Those are three somewhat different, but still full-featured versions of the prayer used in three different Christian localities for community worship. But there are also three other places where the Lord's Prayer is summarized in a single acclamation, *"Abba,* Father!" Think of that as an ecstatic cry similar to a modern one like "Free at last!" That first-century *Abba* Prayer comes from Paul in the mid-50s (Gal. 4:6; Rom. 8:15) and from Mark in the early 70s (14:36). In other words, it is much earlier than those fuller versions in Matthew, Luke, and *The Teaching.* It is, therefore, much closer chronologically to the earlier time and Aramaic language of Jesus than the later Greek versions.

In the earliest transcripts of our New Testament that invocation reads *Abba ho Patēr!* It is bilingual address to God in Aramaic (*Abba*) and Greek (*ho Patēr*). That is significant for three reasons. One is that *Abba* is a more intimate address to God, similar to our "Daddy" rather than our "Father." Another reason is that such a bilingual phrase emphasizes the great transition the Lord's Prayer was undergoing as it moved from the Aramaic-speaking villages of the Jewish homeland to the Greek-speaking cities of the Roman Empire.

A final point concerns how best to render it in English. Since translating it literally as "Father, the Father" sounds strange, translators usually leave it as *"Abba,* Father!" You will notice, however, that the Greek is "the Father" and not just "Father." I would suggest, therefore, that, however we translate it, we should hear it as *"Abba,* THE Father."

We must, I think, take that cry of *"Abba,* the Father!" very, very seriously. I return to it from Mark 14:36 in Chapter 5, but focus here on Paul's almost identical usage in two different letters. How does Paul help us on the interactive relationship of prayer and justice? Does he agree or disagree that prayer to the God of justice above empowers one to divine justice here below?

I opened this chapter with an epigraph from the apostle Paul, "We do not know how to pray as we ought" (Rom. 8:26), and I return to it here, since it is such an extraordinary assertion. Read it first with this emphasis: "*We* do not know how to pray as *we* ought." By using "we" rather than "you," Paul includes himself in the warning. He is writing to the various Christian communities at Rome, a city he has never been to, but soon expects to visit. In that context, and in what turned out to be his final letter, he is not just making a claim about his own prayer or that of his immediate readers. He is making a universal claim about all Christian prayer.

Read it again, but this time with this emphasis: "We do not know *how* to pray as we ought." Paul does not say that we do not know *for what* to pray as we ought. It is not, apparently, that we simply focus on the wrong concerns—on minor over major, on material over spiritual, or on individual over communal matters. The very *how* to pray is unknown to us.

On the other hand, despite this warning about praying, Paul takes it for granted elsewhere that both he and his readers know how to pray. His letters constantly mention that he prays for the recipients, and he asks them to pray for him in return. Think, for example, of his very first letter. "Night and day we pray most earnestly," he tells his audience, "that we may see you face to face and restore whatever is lacking in your faith" (1 Thess. 3:10). Later, the Thessalonian Christians are instructed to "pray without ceasing" (5:17) and asked especially to "pray for us" (5:25). Indeed, even in Romans—the same letter in which he said, "We do not know how to pray as we ought" (8:26)—Paul tells his readers elsewhere to "persevere in prayer" (12:12).

Throughout all of Paul's letters, therefore, from the first one to the last one, we hear this constant refrain: "I pray for you; you pray for me; we all pray for each other." That seems like a mighty amount of praying for Christians who "do not know how to pray," who are, shall we say, prayer-challenged. What does Paul mean by that stunning claim that "we do not know how to pray as we ought"?

Finally, then, what is Paul's own solution to that contradiction between his constant admonitions to pray and this single solemn declaration of the incapacity to do so? He actually gives us his own positive answer on "how to pray" twice, a shorter version in Galatians 4:6–7 and a longer version in Romans 8:14–17. Here is the short one:

God has sent the Spirit of his Son into our hearts, crying, "Abba! Father!" So you are no longer a slave but . . . an heir, through God. (4:6–7)

I proposed earlier that the best way to hold the prayer of the biblical psalms and the justice of the biblical prophets together was this:

we pray to the God of justice to be empowered by that God for justice. But instead of saying that we pray to God for empowerment, Paul says *we are empowered by God to pray*. It is the gift of God's own Spirit that cries out in us, with us, from us, through us: *"Abba,* Father!" So, for Paul, God's own Spirit is the necessary missing element. We cannot pray by ourselves, but only through and by the power of the Holy Spirit. And that ecstatic prayer is the acclamation *"Abba,* the Father," in which all else is already contained.

Furthermore, says Paul, God's Spirit of justice liberates slaves from the bondage of injustice and makes them not only free, but heirs of God. That mention of slavery recalls the liberating God of the Exodus from Egypt in the second book of the Bible. But now it is not just a question of slaves becoming free by the action of God, but of slaves becoming heirs of God.

Is that just a moment of rhapsodic vision that would have to be drastically toned down if and when Paul thought it over? I do not think so, because he says it all again and even more fully in his later letter to the Romans:

> When we cry, "Abba! Father!" it is that very Spirit bearing wit-
> ness with our spirit that we are children of God, and if children,
> then heirs, heirs of God and joint heirs with Christ. . . . The
> Spirit helps us in our weakness; for we do not know how to pray
> as we ought, but that very Spirit intercedes with sighs too deep
> for words. And God, who searches the heart, knows what is the
> mind of the Spirit, because the Spirit intercedes for the saints
> according to the will of God. (8:15–17, 26–27)

All the same language appears here once again: the Spirit of God prays in us and for us; the cry of that Spirit in us is *"Abba,* Father!"; and the result is that we are not just freed slaves of God or even be-loved children of God, but "heirs of God and joint heirs with Christ."

Paul's claim is clear, and it is, as I said, quite stunning. We cannot pray the *Abba* Prayer to God the Father by ourselves or from ourselves.

We can only pray it by, with, and through the Holy Spirit. Better: only the Holy Spirit can pray it in us, for us, and through us. Better still: it is a collaborative prayer between—in this order—God's divine Spirit and our human spirit.

We translate that combination of divinity and humanity—as above—with God's "Spirit bearing witness with our spirit" (8:15). But Paul held the two in a much tighter combination with a single Greek word. He wrote of "with-witnessing" (*summarturei*) to emphasize the extraordinarily profound collaboration between divine Spirit and human spirit in the *Abba* Prayer of Jesus.

One final and all-important question. What does it mean for Christians to become "an heir, through God" (Gal. 4:7) or "heirs of God and joint heirs with Christ" (Rom. 8:17)? We have already seen one aspect of it. God liberates us from injustice and, as heirs, we inherit that same obligation for others. There is, however, another aspect as well, and this goes back to Genesis, the first book of the Bible.

You can see that second aspect if you glance back at the two parts from Romans 8 (vv. 15–17, 26–27) that I cited together above. There is a section of text left out in between—and notice that it is between—those two assertions about the Spirit of God praying within Christians. Here is that magnificent in-between section:

> The *creation* waits with eager longing for the revealing of the children of God; for the *creation* was subjected to futility, not of its own will but by the will of the one who subjected it, in hope that the *creation* itself will be set free from its bondage to decay and will obtain the freedom of the glory of the children of God. (8:19–21)

Christians are called to be heirs not only of God the Liberator, but of God the Creator. We take on God's responsibility for creation itself. If all of that is packed into the very opening *"Abba,* Father!" of the Lord's Prayer, no wonder we cannot pray it of ourselves, but only as empowered by the creative and liberating Spirit of God.

We have now moved beyond any simple ascendancy of prophets over psalms or justice over prayer as some preferential divine option. We have also moved beyond thinking about prayer to God as empowerment by God. Paul has challenged us with the idea that God empowers the very prayer itself.

The *Abba* Prayer as Jesus's great hymn of hope can only be prayed, says Paul, by the Holy Spirit *already* within us and *already* having made us heirs of God and joint heirs (not subheirs, by the way) with and in Christ. That is how we become responsible for healing not only ourselves, but all of creation. But that raises another, even more pressing question. How, then, do we obtain that divine Spirit in the first place? Do we pray for it? Or what do we do?

Actually Paul has been answering that question through all of the preceding chapters of Romans (1–8). Coming from deep within the very core of Jewish tradition, Paul understands God as the God of distributive justice. But, for Paul, that does not primarily mean that God demands us to distribute God's world fairly, justly, and equitably among all God's creatures. It does mean that—but secondarily. Primarily it means that God offers, grants, and distributes God's own identity, character, or Spirit (to use Paul's word) freely, equitably, and justly to all of us.

At this point two physical analogies may be helpful. Think, first, of a heart transplant. After the operation is over, your old, unhealthy heart is completely gone and replaced by a new and healthy one. God, says Paul, offers everyone a graciously free *Spirit transplant*. Our old spirit of bondage to violent injustice is removed and replaced by the Holy Spirit of God's distributive justice and restorative righteousness. But, of course, although a human heart transplant is neither free nor possible for everyone, the divine Spirit transplant is both free and possible for everyone.

Think, next, of a technical rather than a medical analogy. The message on your screen offers you a free—yes, totally free—new operating system (O/S) for your computer. If—but only, of course, if—you hit that "I accept" button, your older operating system will be completely eliminated and the new download will take its place. The free offer becomes a free gift, and all is changed forever.

In Paul's theology only such a O/S change or Spirit transplant empowers us adequately for the making just, or "just-ification"—his term—of God's world, which we have almost destroyed with our lack of "justice"—our "sin," to use his word, once again. But, as always, Paul's vision neither negates nor transgresses human freedom. We and our world are *justified through grace by faith,* says Paul, that is, by the free acceptance of God's free offer.

If we grant Paul all of that, there is one final question. A heart transplant or an O/S change is, after all, an immediate operation. You do not get it piece by piece over weeks, months, or decades. If it happens, it happens all at once. How do we prepare for, maintain, and deepen God's free gift of that Spirit transplant or O/S download?

I return now to where I began this chapter, in the Bible's magnificent book of Psalms. The mysterious secret of prayer is that—like all other human matters—it must mature over time and through practice. And, of course, immaturity is as possible in prayer as anywhere else in our lives. But there is a path forward, because this is how our prayer growth develops:

REQUEST → GRATITUDE → EMPOWERMENT

complaint and petition → thanksgiving and praise → participation and collaboration

There is nothing wrong with prayers of request. There is everything right with taking our hopes and fears under the shadow of transcendence. Neither is there anything wrong—but rather everything right—with prayers of gratitude for the mystery of existence, the challenge of life, and the glory of creation. But it is an immature view of prayer that addresses a Supreme Being radically apart from us who thinks and wills, knows and hears, grants and refuses more or less as we do, but with infinite broadband.

In other words, as Paul says in 1 Corinthians, "When I was a child, I spoke like a child, I thought like a child, I reasoned like a child; when I became an adult, I put an end to childish ways" (13:11). But maturity in prayer—and in theology—means working more and more *from* prayers of request (complaint or petition), *through* prayers of gratitude (thanksgiving or praise), and on *to* prayers of empowerment (participation or collaboration)—with a God who is absolutely transcendent and immanent at the same time. That God is like the air all around us. God, like air, is everywhere, for everyone, always, and both totally free as well as absolutely necessary.

Here are the questions we take from this chapter into the rest of the book. If the "Our Father" is prayed by God's Spirit within and through us, to whom and for what is that prayer uttered? Are we praying for God's intervention, or is God praying for our collaboration? Finally, here is a specific question to lead into the next chapter. If Paul can summarize the entire prayer in its opening cry, "*Abba, the Father!*" how is the rest of that prayer contained in its inaugural address?

2

Our Father in Heaven

Our Father which art in heaven . . .

Matthew 6:9, KJV

Our Father in heaven . . .

Matthew 6:9, NRSV

Her name was Babatha and she lived in Maoza, on the southern tip of Israel's Dead Sea coast. She was illiterate, wealthy, and financially very competent, moving easily within the multiethnic, multicultural, multilingual, and multilegal matrix of Arabs and Jews, Greeks and Romans in her peaceful local world.

Her first husband, Jesus, died in 124 CE, leaving her with an infant son of the same name. She married again, but in 130 CE her second husband, Judah, also died. We know about Judah from an extant contract in which he was lent sixty denarii—at a time when a day's labor cost about one denarius—by the centurion Magonius Valens. He was an officer of the First Thracian Cohort stationed at En-gedi on the mid-western coast of the Dead Sea, and he charged Judah an annual 12 percent interest. But soon afterward, Roman soldiers were no longer lending money to Jewish merchants, as everything changed utterly between Romans and Jews in the Jewish homeland.

In 132 CE Bar Kosiba rose in revolt against Rome, and that peaceful coexistence was brutally shattered, as the legionaries recaptured

Jericho and headed south along the western shore of the Dead Sea. Babatha, along with some friends and relatives, fled south of En-gedi to a cave high on the sheer walls of the Nahal Hever, a narrow canyonlike wadi carved out by the rainy seasons' often violent runoff, but quite dry most of the year.

Babatha and her companions chose a large three-room cave on the northern escarpment of the wadi, while others found hiding in another cave on its southern side. They probably thought the Romans would not find them, or would ignore them, or would be unable to attack them. But the Roman soldiers did find them, and two squads set up their camps—with remnants still visible today—atop both sides of the wadi. They could easily signal across to each other, and they cut off all escape from the caves below. They waited above and starved the refugees to death.

In the 1950s and 1960s Israeli archaeologists excavated the south-side cave, and in that "Cave of Horrors" they found dozens of skeletons—children, women, and men. In 1962 Yigael Yadin explored the northside "Cave of Letters" and found some valuable household utensils and cosmetic items belonging to Babatha. But, then he found her precious legal archives hidden in a crevice and covered with a stone.

The cache of thirty-five documents was wrapped in palm fronds and, for this chapter's overture, I focus on one litigation within it. When Babatha's first husband, Jesus, died in 124 CE, he left four hundred denarii as a trust fund for their infant son, Jesus. Since Babatha was now a widow with a young orphaned son and no patriarchal "protection," the council of the provincial capital at Petra appointed two male guardians to administer the paternal inheritance.

For eight years, from 124 to 132 BCE, Babatha fought those two male guardians in court over the inadequacy of their monthly return from loaning out the money in that fund. They were paying her only an annual 6 percent, when a normal return should have been 12 percent. She claimed that if she herself took over and posted bond for the fund's administration, she could get an annual return of 18 percent. But she never won her case before she ran out of time.

The skeletons of seventeen people were finally found in the "Cave of Letters"—eight women, six children, and three men—and, presumably, Babatha's bones were among them. Despite her undoubted financial competence, she never got her way in a patriarchal world of Roman law. She finally hid her documents beneath that stone in the cave where, again presumably, she met her death.

When, in this chapter, we speak of mothers and fathers, wives and husbands, widows and orphans, patriarchal bias and exclusive language, think always of Babatha as she hovers in the background throughout our discussion. She will be especially present—as a single mother—whenever our biblical texts speak as if the only competent householder is a father or at least a male.

––––––––––

The very first words of the Lord's Prayer are literally "Father of us" in the Greek of Matthew 6:9. It is simply "Father" in Luke 11:2. It was, as we saw in the last chapter, "*Abba,* the Father" in the earlier Aramaic-Greek combination of Paul and Mark. The problem is immediately obvious. How can the "greatest prayer" open with a male-oriented title and a patriarchal mode of address? Why give God a humanlike and male-only name?

Would a nonhuman-like name not be better—say "Spirit," or "Creator," or even simply "God"? And, if one wishes a humanlike title, why not "Mother" rather than "Father" or "Parent" rather than either? Seventy years ago, for example, James Joyce gave us this Islamic-Christian feminine version in *Finnegan's Wake:* "In the name of Annah the Almaziful, the Everliving, the bringer of Plurabilities, haloed be her eve, her singtime sung, her rill be run, unhemmed as it is uneven!" (104.1–3). Whether outside or inside Christianity, how can the "greatest prayer" address God as "Father"?

I grant immediately that "Father" is applied to God from within a traditional and patriarchal society, but in probing that address this chapter considers three points. First, I look at the role and power of metaphor in general, but especially in religion and theology. Can we

ever imagine God except in metaphor—whether it is named or unnamed, overt or covert, conscious or unconscious? And is it not wiser
to have our deepest divine image publicly expressed, so it can be recognized, discussed, criticized, and maybe even replaced? But dare we
replace it without knowing its original meaning and content?

Second, what other equally humanlike and male-oriented names
for God were *not* used when "Father" was chosen? "Father" is not,
after all, the only male image possible in a patriarchal society. What
about God as warrior king, as just judge, or, much later, as feudal
lord? Why "Father"?

Finally, what was the meaning and content of "Father" then and
how should we interpret it today? If we continue to use it, what
should we intend by it? That is surely the most important question.
When the title "Father" was used by Jesus and Paul, what did they
mean by that metaphor?

———

I begin with a consideration of metaphor itself. Metaphor is *seeing as;*
it is imagining and describing one thing as if it were another. Even
before proceeding, notice how weird that is. Why not speak of each
thing as itself? Why not call a spade a spade? Why not always speak
clearly and literally, as we at least attempt to do with food recipes,
road directions, and user manuals? Keep that question at the back of
your mind throughout this section. And keep, along with it, the suggestion of the great Argentinean writer Jorge Luis Borges that "it may
be that universal history is the history of a handful of metaphors."
Is it possible that we can never escape metaphors, the small ones we
readily recognize and the huge ones we do not even notice as such but
simply call reality?

We think we understand metaphor. When we say, "The clouds sail
across the sky," we recognize that we are imagining the sky as sea and
the clouds as sailboats. We would probably be annoyed if a pedantic
literalist said that they were not "sailing," but simply moving. Or if
somebody argued that *As the World Turns* is linguistically more ac-

curate than *The Sun Also Rises*. When a friend collapses into a chair saying, "I'm dead," we do not call either doctor or coroner. We recognize metaphor and would do so even if our friend had announced, "I'm literally dead." But despite, or maybe because of, the daily deluge (yes, there's another metaphor) of standard metaphorical language, strange things happen to our ideas about metaphor as we move into religious, theological, and especially biblical areas.

On the one hand, the seventeenth- and eighteenth-century European Enlightenment (that's a metaphor, by the way) correctly "enlightened" us on the necessity of observation and experimentation in the physical sciences and the value of reason and debate, proof and repetition in science and technology. In that process, the dead hand of inquisitional power and the cold gaze of ecclesiastical control were removed from spheres about which they knew too little and claimed too much. That was a magnificent achievement and must always be appreciated as such.

On the other hand, the Enlightenment also dramatically "endarkened" us on metaphor and symbol, myth and parable, especially in religion and theology. We judge, for example, that the ancients took their religious stories literally, but that we are now sophisticated enough to recognize their delusions. What, however, if those ancients intended and accepted their stories as metaphors or parables, and we are the mistaken ones? What if those pre-Enlightenment minds were quite capable of hearing a metaphor, grasping its meaning immediately and its content correctly, and never worrying about the question: Is this literal or metaphorical? Or, better, what if they knew how to take their foundational metaphors and stories programmatically, functionally, and seriously without asking too closely about literal and metaphorical distinctions?

We have, in other words, great post-Enlightenment gain, but also great post-Enlightenment loss. Is it only poets who know that metaphor is destiny and that literalism has sapped our metaphorical imagination? The late American poet Henry Rago speaks in "The Promising" about "the metaphor not means but end." It is, he reminds us, "Not the technique / But the vocation, the destiny." He also says, in his essay "The Poet in His Poem": "There is the metaphor that is less a metaphor, because it is the metaphor I choose; there is the metaphor that is more deeply, irrevocably a metaphor, because it chooses me."[1] We must be careful, very, very careful about our transcendental metaphors. We do not so much choose them as they do us.

———

I turn next from metaphor in general to metaphor in the New Testament. I begin with some examples concerning Jesus before focusing on God under the metaphor of "Father." My guiding questions are, to repeat, why choose "Father" and what was understood by that specific humanlike and male-oriented title?

First, in the majestic overture of John's gospel, Jesus is named like this: "In the beginning was the Word, and the Word was with God, and the Word was God. He was in the beginning with God. . . . And the Word became flesh and lived among us, and we have seen his glory, the glory as of a father's only son, full of grace and truth" (1:1–2, 14). We will return to that in much fuller detail in Chapter 5, but for now it gives Jesus the title "Word of God." Nobody takes that literally and, however difficult it may be for us to interpret the content of "Word" (*Logos,* in Greek), we know immediately that it is a metaphor.

Next, a few verses later, John the Baptist indicates Jesus as the "Lamb of God" (1:36). Once again, everyone recognizes metaphor there even if, once again, we might still have to debate about how exactly Jesus is a lamb. Does it mean, as Paul says, that Jesus is "our paschal lamb" (1 Cor. 5:7)? Be that as it may, we are certain that it should not be taken literally to mean that Mary had a little lamb.

Finally, a few verses later in John's gospel, a new disciple named Nathanael addresses Jesus as "Son of God" (1:49). With that title, there and throughout the New Testament, the iron grip of literal insistence undermines our metaphorical imagination. In Luke's story of Gabriel's annunciation to Mary, for example, we read: "The Holy

Spirit will come upon you, and the power of the Most High will over-shadow you; therefore the child to be born will be holy; he will be called Son of God" (1:35). Do we interpret that as profound and mag-nificent parable or as actual and factual history? Is it literally about the body of Mary or metaphorically about the status of Jesus? Our post-Enlightenment minds may need some interpretive therapy—like this perhaps: "Let me now," wrote the poet Gerard Manley Hopkins, "Jolt / Shake and unset your morticed metaphors."

I turn now from Jesus to God, and here is my basic principle. There is only one word, term, or title that can ever be used of God literally, and that is "God." Theists may insist that "God exists," and atheists may counter that "God does not exist," but, although the verb "exist" can be used literally of creatures (with or without the negative), it can be used only metaphorically of the Creator. The cloud of unknowing is pierced only by the gleam of metaphor. So our only questions are these: If one speaks of "God," what metaphor is imagined or mentioned, what image is presumed unconsciously or announced consciously? And, furthermore, even if God is mysteri-ously beyond full human comprehension, is it not necessary to name the Holy, is it not required to admit publicly the spirit and charac-ter of one's God?

I grant, of course, that "Father" is a metaphor for God. I also grant that it is a male-oriented metaphor. But that leaves me with this im-mediate and very important question. Is that "Father" intended as an exclusive or inclusive title? Let me explain what I mean by that cru-cial distinction even within male-oriented language.

When you read a sign in a public building that says "Men," you recognize that it is a sign for a bathroom, the term is intended as *exclusive,* and it means "Men Only." Compare that with the announce-ment in our Declaration of Independence that "all men are created equal." That word "men" certainly does not mean "men only," that only "men" were endowed by their Creator with inalienable rights. It is, in other words, intended and should be taken not as an exclusive, but as an inclusive use of male-oriented language. It would, of course,

have been much better if it had said, "all are created equal," just as
our Pledge of Allegiance promises "liberty and justice for all."

A good example of that very basic distinction between exclusive
and inclusive male-oriented language occurs at the start of the Acts
of the Apostles. Luke notes that the Twelve "were constantly devoting
themselves to prayer, together with certain women, including Mary
the mother of Jesus, as well as his brothers" (1:14). But, in the very
next verse, Peter addresses that female and male group as "brethren."
That is intended as *inclusive* language, because "brethren" means all
those present. Therefore, the New Revised Standard Version correctly
retranslates it as "believers."

But when Peter continues and suggests choosing a replacement
for Judas among the Twelve, it must be "one of the *men* who have
accompanied us during all the time that the Lord Jesus went in and
out among us" (1:21). That is intended as exclusive, because for "men"
Luke uses the Greek word "males." For him, the Twelve are the exclusively male twelve apostles.

It is insensitive and inaccurate to address women and men as
"men," but it is discriminatory and oppressive to use "males only"
when that is not physically necessary. In the biblical tradition, before
the New Testament and its Lord's Prayer, is the title "Father" intended
to be exclusive or inclusive?

First, among the Ten Commandments, there is this one: "Honor your
father and your mother" (Exod. 20:12; Deut. 5:16). It does not say,
"obey" your father, but "respect" your mother. It does not make any
hierarchy or even distinction between parents. It commands "honor"
alike to both.

Next, in the biblical book of Proverbs there are over a dozen
cases of father and mother parallelism. Here are two representative
examples:

The father of the righteous will greatly rejoice;
  he who begets a wise son will be glad in him.
Let your father and mother be glad;
  let her who bore you rejoice. (23:24–25)

The eye that mocks a father
  and scorns to obey a mother
will be pecked out by the ravens of the valley
  and eaten by the vultures. (30:17)

The first text has the sequence "father," then "father and mother," and finally mother again as "her who bore you." In the second and not so cheerful one is a representative example of the poetic parallelism of "father" and "mother" found throughout the book of Proverbs.

Finally, that inaugural commandment of honoring one's parents is restated more fully in the Wisdom of Jesus Son of Sirach, also called Ecclesiasticus. This text from the second century BCE is not in the Hebrew scriptures or the Protestant Old Testament, but it is in Roman Catholic and Greek Orthodox Bibles:

Honor your father by word and deed,
  that his blessing may come upon you.
For a father's blessing strengthens the houses of the children,
  but a mother's curse uproots their foundations.
With all your heart honor your father,
  and do not forget the birth pangs of your mother. (3:8–9; 7:27)

The opening verse mentions only "father." But, as it continues, it becomes clear that "father" is not intended as exclusive, meaning "fathers only," but as inclusive, meaning "fathers and mothers." In other words, it intends "parents."

That leads to this next question. As just seen, "father" is often intended in the biblical tradition as an inclusive—even if insensitively male-oriented—shorthand for "father and mother." Is it possible to move any further beyond simply reading "father" and hearing "parent"?

To answer that, I focus next on a series of commands about the observance of the Sabbath that we will see in much greater detail in the next chapter. Here are two examples about the rest commanded for the Sabbath day that ended each week in the biblical tradition:

> Six days *you* shall do *your* work, but on the seventh day *you* shall rest, so that *your* ox and *your* donkey may have relief, and *your* homeborn slave and the resident alien may be refreshed. (Exod. 23:12)

> Six days *you* shall labor and do all *your* work. But the seventh day is a sabbath to the Lord *your* God; *you* shall not do any work—*you*, or *your* son or *your* daughter, or *your* male or female slave, or *your* ox or *your* donkey, or any of *your* livestock, or the resident alien in *your* towns, so that *your* male and female slave may rest as well as *you*. (Deut. 5:13–14)

To whom are those commands addressed? Who is the singular "you" and "your" italicized in those texts? Sons and daughters, homeborn slaves and resident aliens, animals and livestock are all mentioned. If you are thinking within a traditional male-dominated society, you might answer that they are addressed to the fathers and husbands of Israel. *But, if that is so, why are the mothers and the wives not listed in any way?* They are certainly not excluded. So those Sabbath decrees must have been intended for *both* the fathers *and* mothers, for *both* the husbands *and* wives of Israel. That singular "you" and "your" should not be taken exclusively for fathers, but inclusively for parents. But do those same Sabbath injunctions point us beyond even "parents"?

Think once again about Babatha. She is a parent. She is twice widowed. She is a single mother. But she is also a householder. Her precious legal documents show, for example, that she had an arrangement for sharecropping very expensive, very lucrative, and very labor-intensive date-palm groves. Imagine Babatha hearing those Sabbath commandments. She would certainly have considered that she was included in that "you" and "your." She was a mother of Israel, and so she and her household would have observed those Sabbath commands as if they were spoken directly to her.

Those decrees on Sabbath rest are, in fact, addressed specifically not just to fathers or even fathers and mothers, not just to parents, but to householders. They concern not only those with children, but those with land and livestock. They are directed to householders and, indeed, to farmers. Hence, my next question. Does the biblical tradition presume that only males could be householders?

I go back once again to that book of Proverbs, which dates from the sixth century BCE or later. But remember that proverbs are something like the common, everyday, ongoing wisdom of a people. In that text even the "household" belongs to the mother rather than the father. Here are some examples:

There will be enough goats' milk for your food,
 for the food of your household
 and nourishment for your servant girls. (27:27)

She rises while it is still night
 and provides food for her household
 and tasks for her servant girls. (31:15)

She is not afraid for her household when it snows,
 for all her household are clothed in crimson. (31:21)

She looks well to the ways of her household,
 and does not eat the bread of idleness. (31:27)

From all those various biblical examples—from Exodus and Deuteronomy to Proverbs and Sirach—I draw two very important conclusions. One is that, despite its male-oriented prejudice, the biblical term "father" is often simply a shorthand term for "father and mother." In fact, unless context demands exclusive male emphasis, it is usually wiser to presume an inclusive intention.

Another is that "father and mother" does not just intend "parent" in charge of children, but rather "householder" in charge of a home or extended family. The biblical concept of householder does not envisage the single-occupant or even nuclear-family household. It imagines the extended multigenerational household as in those Sabbath day commands. It contains brothers and sisters, unmarried sisters and married brothers, clients and dependents, male and female slaves, animals, lands, and tools.

––––

Hold all of that in mind and return with me to our first chapter. We saw in the prophets that God demands a fair share of God's world for all God's people. We saw in Paul that the gift of God's Spirit makes us heirs of that cosmic responsibility. But where did they get such a radical idea? Where did they get that idea about a fair share for all the people of Israel—let alone for all the people of the world?

The biblical tradition—and maybe the whole human race—knows what a well-run home is like. It knows, therefore, how to recognize a good householder. Walk in and look around. Are the fields well prepared and the livestock well provisioned? Do dependents, from slaves to children, have adequate food, clothing, shelter? Does a sick child get special care? Does a pregnant or nursing mother get special concern? Does everyone have a fair share of everything? Put simply, does everyone have enough?

That basic, domestic model of the good householder, of the just and righteous, fair and equitable householder of the human home, is extended by the biblical tradition to God as Householder of the world house. That is where the biblical writers got it, that is why they are so sure about it, and that is why they believe in it. The well-run household is a microcosm, a miniature of the macrocosm, a well-run world. To call God "Father in Heaven" is to call God "Householder of Earth." And that is why Jesus addressed God as *Abba* in the Lord's Prayer.

———

My next step follows from that basic insight that the father as householder of the home is the model, metaphor, and microcosm for God as the Householder of the World. From the human to the divine, then, what aspects of householder are emphasized in the biblical tradition? There are four main ones.

Householder as Creator. Luke's genealogy of Jesus works backward all the way to creation, and everyone is simply a named "son of" a named father. (Were no females involved as mothers?) And so, in the beginning, Adam was "son of God" (3:38). The father as (pro)creator of the household becomes model and metaphor for God the Creator as divine Father of humanity. Here are two earlier examples, one from the Torah and the other from the Prophets:

Do you thus repay the Lord,
    O foolish and senseless people?
Is not he your father, who created you,
    who made you and established you? (Deut. 32:6)

Yet, O Lord, you are our Father;
    we are the clay, and you are our potter;
    we are all the work of your hand. (Isa. 64:8)

In Genesis God the Creator is imagined through the metaphor of the divine Potter: "The Lord God formed man from the dust of the ground, and breathed into his nostrils the breath of life; and the man became a living being" (2:7). The prophet Isaiah then picks up that metaphor and also equates Creator with Father. The prophet Malachi also asks, "Have we not all one father? Has not one God created us?" (2:10).

Paul also speaks of God as Father-Creator, but watch the parallel structure of this confession in 1 Corinthians:

For us there is one God, the Father,
from whom are all things and *for* whom we exist,
and one Lord, Jesus Christ,
through whom are all things and *through* whom we exist. (8:6)

In other words, for Paul, "a new creation is everything" (Gal. 6:15); and, "if anyone is in Christ, there is a new creation: everything old has passed away; see, everything has become new" (2 Cor. 5:17).

Furthermore, Paul uses "God *the* Father" just a few times, but "God *our* Father" is his more common expression. It appears with ritual regularity in the formulaic greeting at the start of his letters. In his first one he addresses "the Thessalonians in God the Father and the Lord Jesus Christ: Grace to you and peace" (1:1), but, thereafter, it is always, "Grace to you and peace from God our Father and the Lord Jesus Christ" (Gal. 1:3; Phil. 1:2; Philem. 3; 1 Cor. 1:3; 2 Cor. 1:2; Rom. 1:7). God *the* Father as *the* Creator is also God *our* Father as *our* New Creator.

Householder as Protector. Protector is also Savior, Redeemer, and Liberator. The psalmist cries out to "my Father" as "my God, and the Rock of my salvation" (89:26). And the prophet Isaiah proclaims, "You [God] are our Father, our Redeemer from of old is your name" (63:16).

Those titles become clear when you notice the very first time in the Bible that God is imagined as Father. We are accustomed to the story of Moses telling Pharaoh (in God's name), "Let my people go." But God first gives that mission to Moses with these words:

You shall say to Pharaoh, "Thus says the Lord: Israel is my first-born son. I said to you, 'Let my son go that he may worship me.' But you refused to let him go; now I will kill your firstborn son." (Exod. 4:22–23)

That is the very first time the Bible points to God as Father. It is only implicit, of course, in that Israel is God's "firstborn son."

Later in Israel's history that same title of "(firstborn) son" will be given to the monarch. God says of King David, "I will be a father to him, and he shall be a son to me" (2 Sam. 7:14), and of his successor, King Solomon, "He shall be a son to me, and I will be a father to him" (1 Chron. 22:10).

Finally, however, as the Davidic line increasingly failed to fulfill the promises made by God, the prophet Isaiah made this extraordinary correlation of "son" as "father":

> For a child has been born for us,
>   a *son* given to us;
> authority rests upon his shoulders;
>   and he is named
> Wonderful Counselor, Mighty God,
>   Everlasting *Father,* Prince of Peace. (9:6)

The ultimate protector, savior, redeemer, liberator is the Davidic Messiah, who is both Son and Father. And his Household will not be simply a world house. It will be a world house of peace.

Householder as Provider. Society suffers from attacks by outsiders— hence a Protector is needed. But there are also dangers from within the society itself—hence a Provider is also required. One important psalm verse serves as transition from the Householder's role as Protector to that of Provider:

> Father of orphans and protector of widows
>   is God in his holy habitation. (68:5)

But why is God as Father especially concerned with "orphans" and "widows"? Why not all people? Why those ones in particular?

I return to Babatha. After her first husband's death she was a "widow" and her son Jesus was, in the biblical tradition, an "orphan."

For us today, "orphan" is a child lacking both parents, but in that world it meant one without a father. In the book of Lamentations, for example, the prophet Jeremiah mourns the Babylonian destruction of Jerusalem in the early 500s saying, "We have become orphans, fatherless; our mothers are like widows" (5:3).

In a justly run household all will have enough, but there will also be special care and concern for the more vulnerable ones—for the very young or the very weak, for the mentally or physically disabled, and for the temporarily or permanently ill. In the biblical world house of God three major groups are especially defenseless and therefore offered special fatherly care and concern by God as Householder:

- The poor and needy—in a rich society

- Widows and orphans—in a patriarchal society

- Resident aliens—in a tribal society

Those categories come up together again and again like a mantra in warnings from God as Householder:

> You shall not withhold the wages of poor and needy laborers, whether other Israelites or aliens who reside in your land in one of your towns. . . . You shall not deprive a resident alien or an orphan of justice; you shall not take a widow's garment in pledge. (Deut. 24:14, 17)

> Ah, you who make iniquitous decrees,
>   who write oppressive statutes,
> to turn aside the needy from justice
>   and to rob the poor of my people of their right,
> that widows may be your spoil,
>   and that you may make the orphans your prey! (Isa. 10:1–2)

Be a father to orphans,
  and be like a husband to their mother;
you will then be like a son of the Most High,
  and he will love you more than does your mother. (Sir. 4:10)

Those groups are not cases of personal incompetence or individual incapacity. Once again, remember Babatha. She was certainly very, very competent. But, living in a male-dominated society, she was vulnerable to male judges and male trustees and, despite her greater business ability, she could not prevail against them in court.

It is the tribal structure and patriarchal system of a society that make it easy to oppress certain groups, and, therefore, like the weaker members of the family, they are under the very special care of the divine Householder. Those same groups reappear in the New Testament:

Religion that is pure and undefiled before God, the Father, is this: to care for orphans and widows in their distress, and to keep oneself unstained by the world. (James 1:27)

What horrifies the biblical conscience in all those cases is the *inequality* that destroys the integrity of the household and therefore dishonors the Householder. In what sort of household are some members exploited by others? In what sort of household do some members have far less than they want and others far more than they need? What sort of Householder is in charge of such a house?

Householder as Model. In the extended family of the biblical world, daughters and sons learned how to become future householders by implicit and explicit *apprenticeship* to their parents as householders. Female and male householders were their models and paradigms. When, for example, Rebekah "ran and told her mother's household" about the possibility of a marriage with Isaac (Gen. 24:28), it was from her mother's household that she had learned and prepared to have one of her own. "Be like me" was the mantra of that process.

In addition to Creator, Protector, and Provider in the metaphor of God as Father/Householder, Jesus adds another emphasis, namely, the Householder as model. In Matthew's gospel, Jesus gives the Lord's Prayer in the Sermon on the Mount in 6:9–13, that is, almost immediately after his negative admonition about violence and positive one about love in 5:38–48.

First, that section begins with this *negative* command: "I say to you, Do not resist an evildoer" (5:39). That sounds—in English—like total nonresistance or even indifference to evil. But not so in Matthew's Greek. There the verb "resist" is composed of two parts: *anti* and *histēmi*. The major Greek lexicon, Liddell and Scott, explains that verb as meaning: "*to stand against,* especially in battle, *to withstand, oppose.*" It is accurate, I think, to translate Jesus's use in Matthew 5:39 as: "Do not withstand evil *violently.*"

Next, comes the corresponding *positive* command. Jesus presumes that, as in Leviticus, we must "love our neighbor as ourselves" (19:18) and even "love the resident alien as ourselves" (19:34). But this is his striking extension of those passages: "I say to you, Love your enemies and pray for those who persecute you" (Matt. 5:44).

Finally, what is even more striking is *why* we are supposed to act without violence and with love:

> So that you may be children of your Father in heaven; for he makes his sun rise on the evil and on the good, and sends rain on the righteous and on the unrighteous. . . . Be perfect, therefore, as your heavenly Father is perfect. (5:45–46, 48)

God the Father is our model for how to respond to evil against us. That English word "perfect" may also tend to mislead us. Who, we ask, could be "perfect" as God "is perfect"?

The Greek word there is *teleios,* which can certainly be translated "perfect." For example, Jesus tells the rich young man to sell his possessions, give the money to the poor, and follow him, if he "wishes to be perfect" (Matt. 19:21). But there are several different translations of *teleios* elsewhere in the New Testament.

It appears as "complete" (1 Cor. 13:10) or "adult" (1 Cor. 14:20) and especially as "mature" (Phil. 3:15; Col. 1:28; 4:12; Eph. 4:13). The letter of James advises: "Let endurance have its full (*teleion*) effect, so that you may be mature (*teleioi*) and complete, lacking in nothing" (1:4). To be perfect is to be full, complete, mature—qualities the parent models for the child, the householder for the household, and God for all of us.

That is a magnificent vision of loving even one's "enemies," loving even those who hate or persecute, curse or abuse us. It is based on the very character of God as Father or Householder who loves all those in the world house and therefore supplies sunshine for the good and the bad and sends rain on the righteous and the unrighteous alike.

———

Granted that vision of God as Father/Householder who creates, protects, provides for, and models for all in God's household, how does the opening invocation, "Our Father in heaven," relate to the rest of the Lord's Prayer? I answer, for here and now, only in a preliminary way by seeing how the prayer's balanced structure flows from its initial address.

Matthew's version of the Lord's Prayer is a well-crafted, carefully organized, and poetically structured hymn. That means we must pay attention to both form and content. I begin here with a diagram of its skeletal structure, but before looking at it, here are some aspects to focus our understanding.

First, the prayer begins with "Our Father," that is, with a communal "our" rather than just an individual "my." The prayer is certainly "personal," but personal-in-community rather than personal-in-privacy. You may certainly pray it alone, but you are never alone when you pray it.

Second, in the Greek of Matthew, "Our Father" is literally "Father of us." There is no difference in meaning, but "Father / of us" helps us to see immediately the formal division of the prayer into two halves. The former half focuses on the divinity of God; the latter half focuses on our humanity. When you look at the diagram, you will immediately see that pronoun "your"—God's—predominates in the first half, and the pronoun "our" predominates in the second.

Third, as you examine the outline, you will immediately see that there are three units on either side. In the Divinity half are God's name, kingdom, and will. In the Humanity half are our bread, debt, and temptation. Since I have spoken so much about various types of poetic parallelism, what is the point of that threefold balance? Is it just random or accidental? My question is not about the number of units per side, but about the fact that both halves of the prayer have the same number.

Fourth, in the outline I translate phrases from the Lord's Prayer somewhat literally or even woodenly to respect Matthew's intentional emphases and connections. Watch the key words in upper case, whether italicized or not. Notice also how the two halves, Divinity and Humanity, pick up the two parts, "Father / of us," in the Greek of the opening address:

DIVINITY	HUMANITY
in the heavens	*so on earth*
(1) Be hallowed *YOUR* NAME.	(1) Give us this day OUR daily BREAD.
(2) Be come *YOUR* KINGDOM.	(2) And forgive us *OUR* DEBTS, as we also have forgiven *OUR* debtors.
(3) Be done *YOUR* WILL, *as in heaven*	(3) And do not lead *US* into TEMPTATION, but rescue *US* from the evil one.

As already mentioned in the Prologue, the art of the Bible's poetic parallelism is to repeat the same content in slightly different ways, so that the two verses vibrate together like a choral chant. The power of biblical parallelism is that it forces the mind to slow down, to ponder, and to meditate on these questions. Does that second verse add anything to the first one? Do both verses together say something that is not said by either alone?

With that in mind, I wonder if the two balanced sides of the Lord's Prayer intend a certain poetic parallelism? If that is correct, then elegant poetry becomes profound theology. We are dealing with two ways of saying the same thing, two ways of asserting the same challenge. What happens to God and what happens to us are interactive, reciprocal, and collaborative. The priority and sequence are obviously first divinity, then humanity. But can what is said of God happen without us? Can what is said of us happen without God? Can either half of the Lord's Prayer stand alone?

Furthermore, that overall parallelism is underlined in one other way. The opening verse is "Our Father *in heaven*" (literally, "in the heavens"). Next comes mention of God's name, kingdom, and will. Then we have a verse that I cite in the Greek sequence: "as in heaven so on earth." In other words, the first half of the prayer is framed by a phrase about *heaven* and the next half opens with mention of *earth*.

But, once again, each three-unit side is *both* heavenly *and* earthly, each side is *both* divine *and* human. It is not as if God does the first part and we do the second one. Both the divine "Your" and the human "Our" are operative on both sides. It is, to repeat from earlier, a dialectical relationship, like two sides of the same coin, which can be distinguished but not separated.

The hinge of the prayer is "as in heaven so on earth" or, if you prefer the usual translation "on earth as it is in heaven." That centrally key phrase insists on mutuality and reciprocity, on an interaction between the heavenly "Your" of God's name, kingdom, and will and the earthly "Our" of bread, debt, and temptation. And all of these preliminary observations indicate that a careful mind and a poetic soul gave us the present version of the Lord's Prayer in Matthew's gospel.

I make one final point here in preparation for Chapters 3–8. I take very seriously the *greatest commentary,* from Paul, on this *greatest prayer,* from Jesus. Paul's claim in Romans 8:14–17 is that, when the divine Spirit cries out "*Abba,* the Father" in and with our human spirit, we become heirs of God. And, as heirs, we assume the powers and responsibilities of householding our world so that all alike have enough.

Paul was speaking to Christian Jews, and it was quite appropriate to call them "heirs of God" for the care of creation. But is this prayer for Christianity only, or does it speak to all humanity? I suggest that it is a single powerful beat from the heart of biblical tradition and that it is addressed to all the world. I read it, therefore, against this context from Genesis 1:26–28:

> "Have dominion over the fish of the sea, and over the birds of the air, and over the cattle, and over all the wild animals of the earth, and over every creeping thing that creeps upon the earth."
>
> God created humankind in his image,
> in the image of God he created them;
> male and female he created them. . . .
> "Have dominion over the fish of the sea and over the birds of
> the air and over every living thing that moves upon the earth."

That mandate of responsibility is repeated twice to frame and interpret what it means for humans to be made in God's image. Humans ("male and female") are created to run God's world. We are, as human beings, co-responsible with the Householder for the household of the world. Christians are "heirs of God" from Paul, but all humans are "images of God" from Genesis.

I turn next to the rhapsody on that magnificent human destiny in Psalm 8 and, as you read, notice its rampant poetic parallelism:

> When I look at your heavens, the work of your fingers,
> the moon and the stars that you have established;
> what are human beings that you are mindful of them,
> mortals that you care for them?

Yet you have made them a little lower than God,
   and crowned them with glory and honor.
You have given them dominion over the works of your hands;
   you have put all things under their feet,
all sheep and oxen,
   and also the beasts of the field,
the birds of the air, and the fish of the sea,
   whatever passes along the paths of the seas. (8:3–8)

Once again, our human glory is to be "a little lower than God" and thereby responsible for all God's creatures of land, sky, and sea.

Paul interprets the Lord's Prayer to mean that Christians are "heirs of God" with responsibility for the "groaning" of creation. My proposal is that the *Abba* Prayer involves that and much more. It recalls the challenge of Genesis 1:26–28 and Psalm 8, which calls all human beings to that responsibility.

The opening and closing verses of Psalm 8 are verbatim the same: "O Lord, our Sovereign, how majestic is your *name* in all the earth!" (8:1, 9). So, finally, how does what we have learned so far on "Our Father in heaven" prepare for and flow into a discussion of "hallowed be your name"? Why this emphasis on the *name* of God in that context of divine and human responsibility for creation?

The word "name" can mean identity or reputation. Name as *identity* is what is on our credit cards, driver's licenses, and passports. It is what we have in mind when we speak of identity theft as stealing one's name. Name as *reputation* is what we mean when we say somebody has a good name. Your identity is internal to yourself; your reputation is how others see you, judge you, assess you. It is what the biblical book of Proverbs means in this piece of poetic parallelism:

| A | good name | is to be chosen | rather than great riches, |
| and | favor | is better | than silver or gold. (2:1) |

Your good name is the favorable view that others have of you. Name is your reputation or, in other cultures, your face, your countenance, your honor.

The name of God means both God's identity and God's reputation as known externally to human beings in God's world. But why does "hallowed be your name" come immediately after the opening invocation of the Lord's Prayer?

Recall, from earlier in the chapter, what happens when you walk into the house(hold) of another person in the ancient biblical world. How does it look to you? Are fields and flocks, servants and dependents, slaves and aliens, married and unmarried members in good shape? Do all get enough? If all is well, you praise the name, you extol the reputation of the householder.

If, then, you wander the earth seeing God as the world's divine Householder, do you praise God for a job well done? Do you "hallow" the name (reputation) of that God? Or would you like to bluntly say to God, the Father/Householder of the World, "How's that working out for you?"

3

Hallowed Be Your Name

Hallowed be thy name.
> Matthew 6:9, KJV

Hallowed be your name.
> Matthew 6:9, NRSV

From 1965 to 1967 I was studying at the French biblical and archaeological school just north of the Damascus Gate and the Old City of Jerusalem—then in Jordan. It was the École Biblique for short, but we called it the "Cold and Bleak," because its thick stone walls made our rooms totally cool in summer and ditto in winter. We used wooden footrests and fingerless gloves to keep our extremities functional as we worked at our desks. And we brewed strong Arabic coffee to keep warm—coffee with a consistency rather like that of a rubber handball.

For our first study tour we went to Egypt immediately after Christmas in 1965. Our group stayed overnight at Suez and set out in a nine-car caravan the next morning. We crossed the canal on a car ferry around three in the morning, before the first ships were allowed through, and headed south toward Mount Sinai. Our cars, announced as "desert-proof," were aged American ones left over from the 1950s, but kept mobile by superb mechanics. Most of the "road" to Mount Sinai was hard-packed sand, and our caravan stopped every half hour to make certain that the last car was still back there in the dust cloud.

We had permission to stay overnight in a dormitory inside the sixth-century Greek Orthodox monastery of St. Catherine's at the foot of Mount Sinai. Our leader was a Zorba the Greek look-alike who had brought along and would cook all our food during that stay at the monastery. I remember sleeping that night with all my clothes on under the blankets—and still doing a lot of shivering.

We arrived outside the monastery between three and four in the afternoon after a twelve-hour trip from Suez. The sun was already disappearing behind the mountains, and the hot desert day was becoming cold desert night. As we waited for all the cars to arrive, a few of us decided to revisualize the burning bush, when "Moses . . . led his flock beyond the wilderness, and came to Horeb [or Sinai], the mountain of God" (Exod. 3:1). We set a nearby bush on fire. It burned and was consumed. And I move now from the ridiculous to the sublime.

First, when Moses came to Mount Sinai for the first time, he came alone. And what he saw there was a visual paradox, a miraculous contradiction in terms, which, for emphasis, is mentioned twice in the story:

> There the angel of the Lord appeared to him in a flame of fire out of a bush; he looked, and the bush was blazing, yet it was not consumed. Then Moses said, "I must turn aside [from my flock] and look at this great sight, and see why the bush is not burned up." (Exod. 3:2–3)

And that is, of course, the point. It was not just a burned bush— as our silliness had so easily created. It was a *burned but not burned* bush. It was a visual paradox or contradiction in terms. If the bush is burned, it is consumed; if the bush is not burned, it is not consumed. But how can the bush be burned and not consumed, be burned and not burned at the same time? That's like a square circle.

Next, God tells Moses: "Come no closer! Remove the sandals from your feet, for the place on which you are standing is holy ground" (3:5). That command is given between the preceding visual paradox of the mysterious bush and the succeeding verbal one of the mysterious name.

Then God is identified in three ways. First, with regard to the past of the Israelites, God is the God of their ancestors, the Lord of Abraham, Isaac, and Jacob (3:6, 15, 16). Second, with regard to the present, God is the God who will deliver them from "misery" and "sufferings" by taking them "out of Egypt" (3:7–10). Finally, with regard to the future, God promises to bring them "into a land flowing with milk and honey" (3:8, 17). But magnificent as all that is, Moses is not satisfied, and this most fateful interaction takes place:

Moses said to God, "If I come to the Israelites and say to them,
'The God of your ancestors *has sent me to you,*'
and they ask me, 'What is his name?' what shall I say to them?"
God said to Moses, "I AM WHO I AM."
He said further, "Thus you shall say to the Israelites, 'I AM *has sent me to you.*'"
God also said to Moses, "Thus you shall say to the Israelites,
'The Lord, the God of your ancestors . . . *has sent me to you.*'"
(3:13–15a)

As you study that interchange, focus on those three terminal phases "has sent me to you" (italicized for emphasis). You realize that two divine names are held together in tensive interplay. In the center is the name "I AM WHO I AM," and it is framed by the twice repeated other name, "the Lord God of your ancestors." Who is sending Moses and by which name?

The primary and fundamental name of God is a verbal paradox just as the burned-but-not-burned bush is a visual one. God's reply to Moses's question is, in effect: "My name is the unnameable one." But that is a contradiction in terms. It both gives and does not give a name—it is a bush that both burns and does not burn—at the same time. In other words, it is a warning to Moses and us that we cannot ever fully, adequately, or completely name the Holy One. God is fundamentally unnamable. And yet we must always try—the unnameable name must be named, the unburnable bush must be burned, the sacred ground must be walked on—but unsandaled.

That is why, despite that warning, God actually gives Moses a nameable name. That secondary or operational name of God is the God of past, present, and future, the God of tradition and deliverance, indeed, of tradition as deliverance and deliverance as tradition. God is the one who saves God's people from the bondage, misery, and suffering imposed on them by "taskmasters."

There must always be, however, a tension between the primary name—the Unnameable One—and all other names given to God, even that of Deliverer and Savior of God's people. Even that of Father or Householder. On the one hand, we cannot ever *name* the Holy and think we have it done. On the other, we cannot ever *not name* the Holy and think we have it made. That mysterious paradox of God's primary name both produces and subverts, both demands and mutates all of God's other names. How *we* think a deliverer should deliver and a savior save may not be exactly how God delivers and God saves. And that is why we, like Moses, must keep standing on holy ground and must also keep removing our sandals. Not one act or the other, but both together.

With that visit to Sinai as a cautionary overture, I turn back once more to Matthew's version of the *Abba* Prayer of Jesus. We saw its overall structure at the end of the last chapter, recognized its two parallel parts, and noticed how the first part was emphasized as a unit by that triple "your" for God and those framing mentions of "in heaven" (literally, "in the heavens" and "in heaven").

That very deliberate unity is further underlined—in Greek—by having exactly the same format for the three segments:

Be hallowed	the	name	of you
Be come	the	kingdom	of you
Be done	the	will	of you

In the Greek of all our versions, the verb in each line comes first and ends with -*thētō* in rhyming format. That makes the triad sound like a deliberate chant. Next, those three verbs are all in the Greek imperative mood, used for orders and commands, rather than in its optative mood, used for wishes and requests. Furthermore, "hallowed" and "done," in the passive voice, frame the active "come," but the emphasis in all three cases is on God's action.

That is surely extraordinary. And the imperative mood continues throughout the second half of the prayer. Imperatives appear again in "give us," "forgive us," and "deliver us." Should we not have polite requests with "may it be" or at least persistent prayers with "let it happen"? But "be hallowed" and "be come" and "be done" are commands. So who is commanding whom here? Are we ordering God the Father/Householder or is God the Father/Householder ordering us? Or are we, as it were, ordering one another—collaboratively?

I ask one final question on that triple command before concentrating in this chapter on the first one, "hallowed be your name." If all three commands are in such similar format, do they all have exactly the same content? Or is there some deliberate progression from first to second to third challenge?

————

The verb "to hallow" is released from its rather archaic past at least once a year. It is hidden in our trick-or-treat, goblins-and-ghosts festival on October 31 called Halloween. That is short for Hallows' Even or All Hallows' Eve. In the Christian calendar that is the evening before All Saints' Day on November 1. In other words, "hallows" means "saints," and "to hallow" means "to make holy" or "to sanctify."

But here is the question. Persons, places, and things—for example, saints, temples, and scriptures—are called holy because of their relationship with God. How, then, could God ever be other than holy? Is not the name as identity or name as reputation of God always holy? (Is not the Pope always Roman Catholic?) When God's name is hallowed, what exactly is the content of that divine holiness?

The Psalms speak repeatedly of God's "holy name," but as we read through the following examples, is the exact meaning of that holiness evident to us?

Sing praises to the Lord, O you his faithful ones,
    and give thanks to his holy name. (30:4)

Our heart is glad in him,
    because we trust in his holy name. (33:21)

Rejoice in the Lord, O you righteous,
    and give thanks to his holy name! (97:12)

Bless the Lord, O my soul,
    and all that is within me,
    bless his holy name. (103:1)

Glory in his holy name;
    let the hearts of those who seek the Lord rejoice. (105:3)

Save us, O Lord our God,
    and gather us from among the nations,
that we may give thanks to your holy name
    and glory in your praise. (106:47)

My mouth will speak the praise of the Lord,
    and all flesh will bless his holy name forever and ever. (145:21)

If God's name is holy, as those prayers continually proclaim, what exactly is the *precise content* of that holiness?

I begin my search for the meaning and content of God's "holiness" or "hallowedness" with Leviticus 19. Why? Because it opens with God telling Moses: "Speak to all the congregation of the people of Israel and say to them: You shall be holy, for I the Lord your God am holy" (19:2). The rest of that chapter multiplies examples of what *we* must do to be holy, but, because (from that opening verse) God is our model for holiness, they must also indicate—with all due respect—how God is holy. As we saw in the last chapter, the divine Householder is a model for the human householder or, as the Lord's Prayer says, "on earth as in heaven."

One preliminary comment about Leviticus 19 before I focus on God's holiness as reflected in our own and on how that helps us understand "hallowed be your name" in the Lord's Prayer. That chapter is from the Holiness Code of Israel's Priestly tradition. It is therefore no surprise that, unlike the prophetic tradition, seen in Chapter 1, this Priestly tradition resolutely refuses to separate ritual action from distributive justice. Ritual with a God of justice creates and empowers—by interactive covenant—a people of justice. How, then, is divine and human holiness interpreted in Leviticus 19?

First, continuing from that opening command to be holy as God is holy, the chapter repeatedly reminds us of that divine model—with three refrains:

I am the Lord. (8 times: 19:12, 14, 16, 18, 28, 30, 32, 37)
I am the Lord your God. (6 times: 19:3, 4, 10, 25, 31, 34)
I am the Lord your God, who brought you out of the land of
    Egypt. (1 time: 19:36)

We are never allowed to forget divine holiness as a model—or better, empowerment—for human holiness. But notice especially that climactic identification of God as the one "who brought you out of the land of Egypt" (19:36). God is the Deliverer, Redeemer, and Savior of the oppressed. Liberation from Egyptian bondage is, by the way, a constant motivating refrain throughout the book of Leviticus—from 11:45 and 19:34 through 22:33, 43 and 25:38, 42, 55 to 26:13, 45. It is because God acted that way that Israel must act likewise—and be the deliverer of its own oppressed.

Second, here are several examples from Leviticus 19 of how God's deliverance of Israel from Egypt must be continued in Israel's deliverance of its own oppressed:

> When you reap the harvest of your land, you shall not reap to the very edges of your field, or gather the gleanings of your harvest. You shall not strip your vineyard bare, or gather the fallen grapes of your vineyard; you shall leave them for the poor and the alien: I am the Lord your God. (19:9–10)

> You shall not defraud your neighbor; you shall not steal; and you shall not keep for yourself the wages of a laborer until morning. You shall not revile the deaf or put a stumbling block before the blind; you shall fear your God: I am the Lord. You shall not render an unjust judgment; you shall not be partial to the poor or defer to the great: with justice you shall judge your neighbor. (19:13–15)

> When an alien resides with you in your land, you shall not oppress the alien. The alien who resides with you shall be to you as the citizen among you; you shall love the alien as yourself, for you were aliens in the land of Egypt: I am the Lord your God. (19:33–34)

My conclusion, so far, is that, for Leviticus 19, divine holiness models human holiness insofar as *both* maintain distributive justice— especially by delivering the endangered, freeing the oppressed, and protecting the impoverished. That certainly applies to and within Israel, since God says six times, "I am the Lord *your* God." But God also says eight times, "I am the Lord" without any qualification or restriction. Does that apply, then, to the whole world? The answer takes us back from Leviticus 19 to Genesis 1, but still on the trajectory of divine holiness as distributive justice.

———

The link from Leviticus 19 to Genesis 1 comes from a divine command that is made toward the start and then repeated toward the end of Leviticus 19: "You shall keep my sabbaths" (19:3, 30). What do the "sabbaths" (notice that plural) have to do with the holiness of God's name? How does God's Sabbath rest pertain to God's distributive justice?

That question also arises from another point. The verb "hallowed," "sanctified," or "holy-fied" appears on the very first page of our Bible amid multiple emphases on the seventh day, on rest, and on work:

And on the *seventh day*
   God finished *the work that he had done,*
and he *rested* on the *seventh day*
   from all *the work that he had done.*
So God blessed the *seventh day* and hallowed it,
   because on it God *rested* from all *the work that he had done* in
   creation. (Gen. 2:2–3)

Not surprisingly, both Genesis 1 and Leviticus 19 come from the same source within the Torah, namely, the Priestly tradition of Israel. So here is our question: What is the connection between God's holiness, Sabbath holiness, and our holiness? The answer draws us deeper into that magnificent parable about the dawn of creation in Genesis 1:1–2:4a.

Sabbath Creation. In the beginning—as always—is the metaphor. The second parable of creation, in Genesis 2:4b–3:24, imagines God as a divine Potter who creates the first *earthling* (*adam* in Hebrew) by taking *earth* (*adama*), molding it into shape, breathing into it, and creating a "living being" (2:7). But in the first creation parable in Genesis 1:1–2:4a the generative metaphor is quite different. There God is imagined as a divine Architect.

This divine Architect, in creating the "house," splits the work between first *separating and preparing* walls and rooms and then *decorating and filling* those areas with "furniture" and people. The balance of those two operations, the former in 1:3–13 and the latter in 1:14–31, forms the structure of the creation account that starts the Bible's story of our world.

Within that balanced structure, the authors use the same expressions for every "chunk" of creation:

And God said: "Let there be . . ."
> And it was so.
> And God saw that it was good.

That repetition of the same words and phrases makes the first chapter of the Genesis relatively easy when you are first learning Hebrew, but it simply lulls you into a false sense of security that is soon disturbed when you proceed into the rest of the Bible.

When we pay close attention to those repeated expressions, we immediately notice a looming problem. It is an awareness that lets us see into the human mind at work on this chapter. And it confirms that we are dealing with an artistic construction—with, in other words, a parable. The authors know exactly what they are doing. They *know they do not know* how God created the world, but they are equally sure they know its purpose and meaning.

We know their intention, because there are *eight* sets of those fixed formulas, eight sets that begin with "And God said: 'Let there be . . .'" There are, in other words, eight chunks of stuff to be created. And there is the problem. It looks like we are going to get a week of eight days and a Sabbath on the ninth. And that is where we see the authors swerve—quite openly and obviously—and thereby reveal—quite openly and obviously—the consciously artificial and intentionally parabolic purpose of the creation account that begins the Torah and the Bible.

What they do is "squeeze" eight chunks of stuff and eight sets of formulaic phrases into six days by having one set apiece on Days 1 and 4, 2 and 5, but two sets on Days 3 and 6, as you can easily see in the accompanying chart. Furthermore, the fourth and final chunk of creation in the "separating and preparing" half of creation (plants, trees) is "squeezed" in there, although it more properly belongs in the second "decorating and filling" half.

All of that is important only to emphasize the self-conscious deliberation and magnificent *art*-ificiality that went into those balanced halves. Creation is, for the Priestly tradition, a beautifully balanced divine masterpiece.

The First Creation Account

Separating and Preparing

Day 1

(1) *Then God said, "Let* [LIGHT] *be."*

And there was [LIGHT].
And God saw that it was good.
And there was evening and there
   was morning, the first day.
   (1:3–5)

Day 2

(2) *And God said, "Let* [SKY] *be."*

And it was so.

And there was evening and there
   was morning, the second day.
   (1:6–8)

Day 3

(3) *And God said, "Let* [SEA, LAND]
   be."
And it was so.
And God saw that it was good.
(4) *Then God said, "Let* [PLANTS, TREES]
   be."
And it was so.
And God saw that it was good.

And there was evening and there
   was morning, the third day.
   (1:9–13)

Decorating and Filling

Day 4

(5) *And God said, "Let* [SUN, MOON]
   be."
And it was so.
And God saw that it was good.
And there was evening and there
   was morning, the fourth day.
   (1:14–19)

Day 5

(6) *And God said, "Let* [BIRDS, FISHES]
   be."

And God saw that it was good.
And there was evening and there
   was morning, the fifth day.
   (1:20–23)

Day 6

(7) *And God said, "Let* [ANIMALS] *be."*

And it was so.
And God saw that it was good.
(8) *Then God said, "Let* [HUMANS] *be."*

And it was so,
God saw everything ... was very
   good.
And there was evening and there
   was morning, the sixth day.
   (1:24–31)

In that structure, Days 1 and 4, Days 2 and 5, and Days 3 and 6 correspond to one another. But although Days 1, 2, 4, and 5 each have one chunk of creation and one set of formulaic expressions apiece, Days 3 and 6 have two chunks of creation and two sets of formulaic expressions apiece.

It is that compression of eight chunks into six days that clarifies the authors' intention and purpose. Put negatively, we humans are not the crown of creation. (We are the work of a late Friday afternoon. And maybe not even God's best work is done on a late Friday afternoon.) Put positively, the crown of creation is the Sabbath day itself.

Creation is not the work of six days, as is often mistakenly said—and whether it is said literally or metaphorically, historically or parabolically, it is still mistaken. Creation is the work of seven days, and, as its climax, the Sabbath day is built into the very fabric of our world, the very creation of our earth. That is why, as we see below, the Sabbath(s) will be so important for understanding the holiness of God and what it means to make and keep holy the name of that God.

Finally, one last point before continuing the Leviticus 19 lead that sent us to Genesis 1. In that ecstatic vision of the dawn of creation there is no bloodshed—not between animals, not between animals and humans, and not between humans:

> God said, "See, I have given you every plant yielding seed that is upon the face of all the earth, and every tree with seed in its fruit; you shall have them for food. And to every beast of the earth, and to every bird of the air, and to everything that creeps on the earth, everything that has the breath of life, I have given every green plant for food." And it was so. (1:29–30)

We may smile at that dream of lions on lettuce, tigers on tofu, and panthers on pesto. But, rather than mocking carnivores as would-be herbivores, what about humans not killing one another? Animals have instinct, and we have conscience. We left Eden in Genesis 2–3 having eaten of "the tree of the knowledge of *good and evil*" (2:17), that is, with only conscience as our guide. Our first act out of Eden was fratricidal murder and escalating violence in Genesis 4 (more on that in Chapter 8).

Be that as it may, what does God's Sabbath—in Leviticus 19 or Genesis 1—have to do with God as the Holy One of justice and righteousness? It is time to follow the trail from Sabbath day through Sabbath year to Sabbath jubilee. And always remember that, from Genesis 1 onward, that Sabbath regulates the weekly structure of our temporal world. What, then, is the purpose of God's Sabbath?

Sabbath Day. The Jewish Sabbath on Saturday simply developed, we might think, into the Christian Sabbath on Sunday. It was only, we might think, a change of day. Sunday is a day of rest, so that Christians may attend church. It is rest from work *for* worship. But the original Sabbath was rest from work *as* worship.

Here are three examples from the Torah—still, by the way, in our Christian Old Testament—that bespeak a very different religious sensibility, a very different meaning for the Sabbath day:

> Remember the sabbath day, and keep it holy. Six days you shall labor and do all your work. But the seventh day is a sabbath to the Lord your God; you shall not do any work—you, your son or your daughter, your male or female slave, your livestock, or the alien resident in your towns. For in six days the Lord made heaven and earth, the sea, and all that is in them, but rested the seventh day; therefore the Lord *blessed* the sabbath day and *consecrated* it. (Exod. 20:8–11)

> Six days you shall do your work, but on the seventh day you shall rest, *so that* your ox and your donkey may have relief, and your homeborn slave and the resident alien may be refreshed. (Exod. 23:12)

> Observe the sabbath day and keep it holy, as the Lord your God commanded you. Six days you shall labor and do all your work. But the seventh day is a sabbath to the Lord your God; you

shall not do any work—you, or your son or your daughter, or your male or female slave, or your ox or your donkey, or any of your livestock, or the resident alien in your towns, *so that* your male and female slave may rest as well as you. Remember that you were a slave in the land of Egypt, and the Lord your God brought you out from there with a mighty hand and an outstretched arm; therefore the Lord your God commanded you to keep the sabbath day. (Deut. 5:12–15)

That is all addressed, as we saw in Chapter 2, to the householders of Israel—both men and women—concerning the Sabbath day in their homes. It applies to everyone, including work animals, slaves, children, and resident aliens.

Furthermore, "blessed" and "consecrated" in Exodus 20:11 repeat the same Hebrew and Greek verbs as "blessed" and "hallowed" seen earlier in Genesis 2:3. The Sabbath makes holy, hallows, sanctifies, and consecrates the entire creation, because it places the justice of equality as the crown of creation. Not only the householders, but everyone—animals, slaves, children, dependents—must all get an equal day of rest from work.

To emphasize that meaning, I have italicized "so that" in the last two texts, because it gives the purpose and intention of those divine commands. Everyone alike must get a rest from work and must get it not at the householder's pleasure or whim, but because it is built into the rhythmic measure of time, is in fact the primary regulator of weekly time.

The Sabbath day has nothing to do with freedom from work *so that* one may go to some place of worship. It is about the distributive justice of rest from work for all who work as worship itself. It is public manifestation of God's very character as the Just One, because it comes with God's creation itself.

Sabbath Year. We are still following the Sabbath process as it turns time itself into both symbol and example of divine justice, following Sabbath day, Sabbath year, and Sabbath jubilee as they establish and hallow, respectively, the weeks, the years, and the centuries of human time upon this earth. The Sabbath year is celebrated, of course, every seventh year. Aspects of liberation or deliverance are associated with it: resting the land, remitting debts, and freeing debt slaves. I consider only the first one here and reserve those other two for Chapter 7, when we consider "Forgive us our debts" in the Lord's Prayer.

Two rather different versions of the Sabbath year's "rest" for the land and its purpose appear in Exodus 23 and Leviticus 25. We must be careful not to read the latter back into the former. Here is that earlier vision:

> For six years you shall sow your land and gather in its yield;
> but the seventh year you shall let it rest and lie fallow, *so that*
> the poor of your people may eat; and what they leave the wild
> animals may eat. You shall do the same with your vineyard, and
> with your olive orchard. (Exod. 23:10–11)

For six years, it says, the land may be worked, and the produce gathered in as harvest. But during the seventh year, what it produces is to be left for poor people and wild animals.

On the one hand, this is but a seventh-year extension of the yearly command to leave the corners of the fields and the gleanings or leftover spills of the harvest: "When you reap the harvest of your land, you shall not reap to the very edges of your field, or gather the gleanings of your harvest; you shall leave them for the poor and for the alien: I am the Lord your God" (Lev. 23:22).

On the other hand, it is very hard to imagine every field in the entire land treated like that every seventh year. What was probably expected was a field rotation, so that one-seventh of one's produce went to the poor every year. The corners of the fields and the gleanings of the harvest *belonged* by divine law to the poor, as did one-seventh of what the land produced.

But if it is hard to imagine Exodus 23 in practice, it is almost impossible to do so for Leviticus 25:

When you enter the land that I am giving you, *the land shall observe a sabbath for the Lord.* Six years you shall sow your field, and six years you shall prune your vineyard, and gather in their yield; but in the seventh year there shall *be a sabbath of complete rest for the land,* a *sabbath for the Lord:* you shall not sow your field or prune your vineyard. You shall not reap the aftergrowth of your harvest or gather the grapes of your unpruned vine: it shall be *a year of complete rest for the land.* You may eat what the land yields during its sabbath—you, your male and female slaves, your hired and your bound laborers who live with you; for your livestock also, and for the wild animals in your land all its yield shall be for food. (25:2b–7)

Here the land is to be left fallow, so that the land itself has a rest; there is to be no work on cereals or vines. Nothing, you will note, is said about the poor. That is so incredible that Leviticus has to answer the obvious objection that it would result in massive starvation:

Should you ask, "What shall we eat in the seventh year, if we may not sow or gather in our crop?" I will order my blessing for you in the sixth year, so that it will yield a crop for three years. When you sow in the eighth year, you will be eating from the old crop; until the ninth year, when its produce comes in, you shall eat the old. (25:20–22)

Like the Sabbath creation that crowned a world where blood never defiled the land in Genesis 1:29–30, this Sabbath year is absolutely utopian and deliberately impractical. The Priestly tradition was not interested in crop rotation, agricultural management, or responsible farming. It was intended as shock treatment, to make the hearers realize that God's land was a living thing and to make them ponder its right to have a rest like everything else in God's creation.

It is, once again, not about agricultural wisdom, but about distributive justice—for the land itself, the inhabitants, the domestic animals, and the wild animals. It applies, furthermore, across the great Mediterranean triad of grains, olives, and vines.

The logic of all these Sabbath injunctions is an attempt to return once more to that beginning moment of Sabbath creation, when all the world was distributed fairly and equitably by God and was declared good and blessed in its inaugural glory. And so, immediately after the Sabbath year in Leviticus 25:1–7 comes the Sabbath jubilee in Leviticus 25:8–55.

Sabbath Jubilee. "Ah, you who join house to house," warned the prophet Isaiah, as we saw earlier, "who add field to field, until there is room for no one but you, and you are left to live alone in the midst of the land" (5:8). But how do you stop that process of ever increasing inequality? Like this:

> You shall count off seven weeks of years, seven times seven years, so that the period of seven weeks of years gives forty-nine years. Then you shall have the trumpet sounded loud; on the tenth day of the seventh month—on the day of atonement—you shall have the trumpet sounded throughout all your land. And you shall hallow the fiftieth year and you shall proclaim liberty throughout the land to all its inhabitants. (Lev. 25:8–10a)

This establishes a super-Sabbath, as is clear from all those multiplied sevens. It is also the climax of the entire Sabbath process of restoring justice and righteousness that runs through the Torah from Genesis to Leviticus. That is why that jubilee year starts on the Day of Atonement. It is an attempt—every half century—to atone for what has happened to the holy land of a holy God. As always, holiness means the justice of a fair distribution for all, the justice of an equitable household:

> It shall be a jubilee for you: you shall return, every one of you, to your property and every one of you to your family. That fiftieth year shall be a jubilee for you: you shall not sow, or reap the

aftergrowth, or harvest the unpruned vines. For it is a jubilee; it shall be holy to you: you shall eat only what the field itself produces. In this year of jubilee you shall return, every one of you, to your property. (Lev. 25:10b–13)

The word "jubilee'" is Hebrew, but in the Greek Old Testament it is translated as "forgiveness" in the sense of debt release, remission, freedom, liberty. We will, of course, find the term again later in "Forgive us our debts" from the Lord's Prayer in Chapter 7.

The purpose behind the Sabbath jubilee of forgiveness is to return all alienated property to its original familial ownership. But why must that happen? "The land shall not be sold in perpetuity," God says a few verses later, "for the land is mine; with me you are but aliens and tenants" (25:23). As resident aliens and tenant farmers we cannot buy and sell land at all; nor can we even mortgage or foreclose on it permanently. Since God's inaugural distribution to the tribes and families of Israel was fair and equitable, the Sabbath jubilee seeks to restore that original situation.

Maybe that was only utopian thinking, nothing but idle dream and ideal law? Was it ever observed regularly every fifty years? Probably not. And if it was, how could it have been administered? Great nations can proclaim that all are "created equal" and never accomplish that vision; they can train their children to pledge allegiance to "liberty and justice for all" despite what is all around them. Still, then and now, how have Jews and Christians decided—without explanation or justification—that the Sabbath jubilee can be serenely ignored?

———

Name is about face, countenance, honor, or public reputation. But in the biblical world—and others like it—reputation was one's deep identity rather than one's surface image. God's name is God's character and identity as publicly acknowledged in the world. It is, the Bible insists, a holy name, but that does not give us any immediate content for divine holiness—or for human holiness on the model of God's. Does not every religion consider as holy the name of its God?

All that we have seen so far—from Leviticus 19 to Genesis 1 and from Sabbath day through Sabbath year to Sabbath jubilee—proclaims that the holy name and divine reputation of the biblical God concerns distributive justice and restorative righteousness and that our holiness is a participation in that divine character, identity, and name.

I began this chapter with the visual paradox of God's burned but unconsumed bush and the corresponding verbal paradox of God's named but unnameable identity. Moses was told that, despite having an utterly and absolutely mysterious name, God was to be known as the Deliverer of the oppressed: "I have observed the misery of my people who are in Egypt; I have heard their cry on account of their taskmasters. Indeed, I know their sufferings, and I have come down to deliver them" (Exod. 3:7–8). God the Deliverer from injustice said, "This is my name forever, and this my title for all generations" (3:15).

Next I asked how God's name is made holy or hallowed, and I followed that question from Leviticus 19 back to Genesis 1. In that former text the holiness of God was mirrored in the holiness of God's people, and both types of holiness meant—no surprise after Exodus 3—deliverance of the oppressed, the impoverished, and the defenseless. In that latter text, the holiness of the Sabbath day, that is, the justice of an equal rest for all, came from creation itself. It was not just a cultic mandate for Israel, but a challenge of distributive justice for all the world.

Where do we go from here? In the Lord's Prayer how does "Your kingdom come" flow from the preceding "hallowed be your name"? Does it go beyond it or simply repeat it—even if with different words? It goes beyond it by suggesting how God's name as the one who delivers from oppression becomes operative for the whole world.

The next chapter, on "Your kingdom come," shows that the biblical tradition, which flowed through Jesus into his *Abba* Prayer, presents an alternative to the violent normalcy of our world and a different vision for peace on our earth.

4

Your Kingdom Come

Hesiod was a Greek pessimist for whom the wineglass of history was half empty—and getting emptier. Around the start of the seventh century BCE his *Works and Days* proposed that humanity had gone through five great ages or stages—but in ever descending order. The Gold, Silver, Bronze, and Heroic Ages yielded finally to his own contemporary Iron Age. "I wish that I were not any part of the fifth generation," he said. "It has no place for the righteous and the good," but instead "gives praise to violence and the doer of evil" (175, 191).

Aemelius Sura was a Roman optimist for whom the wineglass of history was half full—and getting fuller. Around the middle of the second century BCE he proclaimed, according to Velleius Paterculus's *Compendium of Roman History,* that "the Assyrians were the first of all races to hold world power, then the Medes, and after them the Persians, and then the Macedonians. Then . . . the world power passed to the Roman people" (1.6). The five great ages of the world are now five great empires, with Rome as their climax. The gods had "exalted this great empire of Rome to the highest point yet reached on earth," so that it had become "the empire of the world" (2.131).

Daniel was a Jewish realist for whom the wineglass of history was not so much half empty or half full as cracked, leaking badly, and in serious need of repair. Also around the mid-second century BCE, he agreed with Sura that four great imperial kingdoms had preceded their own time, but he proposed a very different fifth one as their climax. It was not the kingdom of Rome, but rather the kingdom of God. And it stood against all imperial kingdoms before, during, or after its advent.

That is the message from a nighttime vision in the book of Daniel: "The God of heaven will set up a kingdom that shall never be destroyed, nor shall this kingdom be left to another people. It shall crush all these kingdoms and bring them to an end, and it shall stand *forever*" (2:44).

In the biblical book of Daniel the four preceding empires are those of the Babylonians, Medes, Persians, and Macedonian Greeks. They are represented as beasts "up out of the sea," feral thrusts from the chaos of the land-threatening ocean (7:3). The Babylonian Empire "was like a lion and had eagles' wings"; the Median Empire "looked like a bear"; and the Persian Empire "appeared like a leopard" (7:4–6).

No comparison with a known wild animal, however, is adequate to describe the fourth imperial kingdom, of the Macedonian Greeks. It is like nothing that came before it. Daniel can only call it dreadfully "different," and he does so three times:

> [It was] terrifying and dreadful and exceedingly strong. It had great iron teeth and was devouring, breaking in pieces, and stamping what was left with its feet. It was *different* from all the beasts that preceded it. . . . [It] was *different* from all the rest, exceedingly terrifying, with its teeth of iron and claws of bronze, and which devoured and broke in pieces, and stamped what was left with its feet. . . . [It was] *different* from all the other king-

doms; it shall devour the whole earth, and trample it down, and break it to pieces. (7:7, 19, 23)

This is the fourth-century BCE empire of Alexander the Great, whose infantry carried two-handed twenty-foot pikes. That length meant about five ranks of pike heads pushing their lethal tips past one another into the killing zone. With heavy infantry as anvil and heavy cavalry as hammer, Alexander's terrible war machine swept across "the whole earth."

Those imperial kingdoms are animal-ified (not person-ified!) as "beasts" from the disorder of the sea's fury. By contrast the fifth kingdom is personified "like a son of man" from the order of God's heaven (7:13). That gives us two expressions requiring some explanation: "son of man" and "kingdom of God."

Son of Man. In male chauvinistic usage in English, "humanity" may be rendered as "mankind," and "human beings" as "men." In male chauvinistic usage in Hebrew or Aramaic "human being" may be termed "man" or "son of man." For example, the King James Bible translates the poetic parallelism in Psalm 8:4 literally: "What is man, that thou art mindful of him? and the son of man, that thou visitest him?" But the New Revised Standard Version translates it: "What are human beings that you are mindful of them, mortals that you care for them?" What is at stake in Daniel behind that "son of man" language? It is this: the first four empires—that is, all previous ones—are inhuman; only the fifth and final empire is truly human.

The fifth kingdom, the kingdom of God, is brought down from heaven to earth by a transcendental Human One who has been entrusted with it by God, the transcendent Ancient One (7:9–13). Daniel 7 mentions this three times for emphasis:

To *him* was given dominion and glory and kingship, that all peoples, nations, and languages should serve him. His dominion is an everlasting dominion that shall not pass away, and his kingship is one that shall never be destroyed. (7:14)

The holy ones of the Most High shall receive the kingdom and possess the kingdom forever—forever and ever. (7:18)

The kingship and dominion and the greatness of the kingdoms
under the whole heaven shall be given to *the people of the holy ones
of the Most High;* their kingdom shall be an everlasting kingdom,
and all dominions shall serve and obey them. (7:27)

There are two significant emphases in those repetitions. One is
that the transcendent "humanlike one" is both the guardian and the
personification of God's kingdom. The "beastlike" ones are imperial
kings who represent imperial kingdoms—compare the "four kings"
of 7:17 with the four "kingdoms" of 7:23. The "humanlike one" represents God's kingdom. It is given to "him" in 7:14, but for all God's
"people" in 7:18, 27.

The other point is that triple emphasis on "everlasting." Imperial
kingdoms come and go, rise and fall, but God's kingdom is an "everlasting" one. This is emphasized as well in earlier chapters of Daniel:
"His kingdom is an *everlasting* kingdom, and his sovereignty is from
generation to generation" (4:3); "His sovereignty is an *everlasting* sovereignty, and his kingdom endures from generation to generation"
(4:34); "His kingdom shall never be destroyed, and his dominion has
no end" (6:26).

Kingdom of God. The second term—after "son of man"—that requires some preliminary explanation is "kingdom of God."

Daniel 7 places beastlike kingdoms *versus* a humanlike kingdom,
earth-born kingdoms *versus* a heaven-born kingdom, and, as earlier
in Daniel, transient kingdoms *versus* an everlasting kingdom. But
we are not told exactly how this kingdom of God is internally different from those kingdoms. They are given external qualifications,
but not internal descriptions. So far that confrontation is emphatic
enough, but what—beyond name-calling—is the intrinsic difference
in content?

When, for example, the *Abba* Prayer commands the Householder of the world house, "Your kingdom come," how precisely does it—and did Jesus—imagine this kingdom of God in content, mode, and method? And how does it differ from the first-century kingdom of Rome? For over a century and a half before that time both the kingdom of Rome and the kingdom of God had both, as just seen, claimed to be the climactic fifth—and therefore final— kingdom of earth. But what—beyond claim and counterclaim—is the difference between them?

One preliminary point. What about that rather outmoded term "kingdom"? I was born a citizen of Ireland, for example, and am now a citizen of the United States. Both those countries struggled successfully to free themselves from the same king-led empire. Why, then, would I or anyone else today want to speak of the "kingdom" of God in the Lord's Prayer? Would it not be better to speak of the people of God, the community of God, the kinship of God, or, especially, the household of God? Why continue to accept such an antique and male-focused expression as "kingdom"? There are two main reasons.

One reason is that retaining "kingdom" but qualifying it as divine is a way to show that it clearly, directly, and explicitly opposes all those earthly imperial kingdoms. It intends to present a specific alternative option to the imperialism that has been for so long the normalcy on earth. Another reason is that God's kingdom is not just about interior and individual religion. It certainly includes that aspect, but only within the wider aspect of exterior and communal and—dare we say the word?—*organized* religion.

But even if tradition demands that we keep the term "kingdom," we must certainly understand it as the biblical tradition and the Lord's Prayer intended it. Like this. Our English word "kingdom" translates the Hebrew *malkuth* and the Aramaic *malkutha*. Both those words emphasize process over person and style of rule over area of control. You could more accurately translate them as the "reigning" of God rather than the "kingdom" of God, because they stress the type and mode of divine rule—as distinct from the type and mode of imperial rule. The Greek equivalent is the feminine noun *basileia* and, once again, what is underlined is not so much *where* God rules the world as *how* God rules the world.

When you read "kingdom of God," therefore, mentally rephrase it as the "ruling style of God." It imagines how the world would be if the biblical God actually sat on an imperial throne down here below. It dreams of an earth where the Holy One of justice and righteousness actually gets to establish—as we might say—the annual budget for the global economy. (By the way, the word "economy" comes from the Greek words *oikos,* "household," and *nomos,* "law." "Economy" means the law of the household.)

———

Deep below our geological earth are giant tectonic plates that grind against one another along fault lines and produce the surface disturbances of volcanoes, earthquakes, and tsunamis. Deep below our historical world are the tectonic plates of *empire* and *eschaton,* and we have just seen their seismic clash in Daniel 7.

Empire is easy enough to understand. It has been the way of the world throughout the last six thousand years of recorded history. We can trace imperialism back to the invention of irrigated agriculture on the floodplains of rivers like, for example, the Tigris and Euphrates in Mesopotamia (modern Iraq). Annual snowmelts from distant mountains sent rich alluvial sediment downstream, and irrigated farming enhanced by dikes and canals vastly increased fertility, prosperity— and population. We call it the Neolithic, or New Stone Age, Revolution. We also call it the dawn of civilization.

With that magnificent Mesopotamian dawn we got not only irrigated farming, but also written records, walled cities, and permanent temples. We also got control and manipulation of grains, animals— and people—since irrigation demands organization of the many by the few. We also got imperialism. As prosperity and population increased, the farmer "haves" pressed outward and the nomad "have-nots" pressed inward. How far, then, would borders have to extend to ensure safety and security? Outward, ever outward—maybe outward to the whole world. The dawn of civilization was also the birth of empire.

Eschaton is not quite so easy to understand. The Old Testament's *faith* was that God was just, in control of the world, and in covenant with Israel to establish justice worldwide. But the Old Testament's *experience* was that the world was unjust and under the control of evil, and that Israel received far more than its fair share of oppressive violence. How could you possibly reconcile that faith and that experience? By *eschaton*?

The word *eschaton* is an ordinary Greek word for "the end." So its meaning always depends on context. The end, yes, but the end of what? First, a negative. It is not—emphatically not—about the end of the world. That unfortunate misunderstanding arises especially from reading Matthew, who speaks a few times about "the end of the world" (13:39, 49; 24:3, 20) in the King James Version. But his Greek term is actually not "world" (*kosmos*), but "age" (*aiōn*)—Matthew refers to the end of this age, period, or time of evil, war, violence, injustice, and oppression. Hence the New Revised Standard Version correctly translates Matthew's Greek as "the end of the age."

The *eschaton* is not about the destruction of the world, but about its transformation into a place of justice and nonviolence. It is not about the annihilation of the earth, but about its transformation into a location of freedom and peace. Daniel's vision of the kingdom of God coming down from heaven to earth was an *eschatological* vision, and my own term for that is the *Great Divine Cleanup of the World*. Here is how that future is imagined in four texts, three from the Bible and a final one from outside it.

First, God's Great Cleanup establishes worldwide *peace*. Recall those famous lines found verbatim in two separate biblical books: "They shall beat their swords into plowshares, and their spears into pruning hooks; nation shall not lift up sword against nation, neither shall they learn war any more; but they shall all sit under their own vines and under their own fig trees, and no one shall make them afraid" (Mic. 4:3–4; Isa. 2:4).

Next, God's Great Cleanup establishes a worldwide *banquet*. There will be "for all peoples a feast of rich food, a feast of well-aged wines, of rich food filled with marrow, of well-aged wines strained clear. . . . Then the Lord God will wipe away the tears from all faces, and the disgrace of his people he will take away from all the earth" (Isa. 25:6, 8).

Finally, God's Great Cleanup establishes worldwide *equality*. I cite here a text from outside the Bible because, unlike those preceding prophetic texts, this one comes from the same time as Jesus. "The earth will belong equally to all, undivided by walls or fences. . . . Lives will be in common and wealth will have no division. For there will be no poor man there, no rich, and no tyrant, no slave. Further, no one will be either great or small anymore. No kings, no leaders. All will be equal together" (*Sibylline Oracles* 2.319–24).

Two other terms often associated with God's eschatological transfiguration of the world will be important for understanding exactly what the *Abba* Prayer of Jesus means by "Your kingdom come" as we continue through this chapter. They are *apocalypse* and *messiah*.

The word *apocalypse* comes from Greek and means a revelation about the *eschaton*. In Daniel 7, for example, the seer has an apocalyptic revelation. It begins by saying that "Daniel had a dream and visions of his head as he lay in bed" (7:1). Later his dream vision is explained by an angelic interpreter: "As for me, Daniel, my spirit was troubled within me, and the visions of my head terrified me. I approached one of the attendants to ask him the truth concerning all this. So he said that he would disclose to me the interpretation of the matter" (7:15–16).

Notice one special aspect of the term *apocalypse* (or *apocalyptic*). In itself, it could apply to *any* revelation about the Great Divine Cleanup of the World. But empires had been steadily getting more powerful and now, in the first century CE, Rome was the most powerful empire the world had ever known. In that context, apocalypse emphasized revelation about the imminence, the any-day-now-ness of God's transformative advent. If not now, when? If not now, why not?

The word *messiah* in Hebrew becomes *Christos* in Greek. It means God's "anointed" agent for that *eschaton*. In Daniel 7, for example, that transcendental Human One ("one like a son of man") who brings God's kingdom down from heaven to earth for God's people is one such messianic figure. But that term requires more detailed consideration, since Jesus was accepted by those first Messianic or Christian Jews as the Messiah, or Christ.

———

When the *eschaton* dawned, when the kingdom came, when the Divine Cleanup began, would God do everything by direct and immediate divine intervention? Would the *eschaton* be, as it were, a lightning strike of divine power? Or would God use some intermediary? If so, what would that messianic agent of transformation be like? Would it be angelic or human and, if human, would it be an anointed priest, an anointed prophet, or an anointed king?

The domestic householder's fair administration of the house was, as we saw in Chapter 2, the great model for the divine Householder's just administration of the world house:

Mighty King, lover of justice, you have established equity; you have executed justice and righteousness in Jacob. (Ps. 99:4)

I am the Lord; I act with steadfast love, justice, and righteousness in the earth, for in these things I delight, says the Lord. (Jer. 9:24)

In Israel's ongoing experience, however, that notion of "household" extended not only from the *peasant's farm as house* to *God's world as house*. In between, it was also applied to the *king's land as house*, since the king was the divinely appointed householder of God's land:

Blessed be the Lord your God who has delighted in you [King Solomon] and set you on the throne of Israel! Because the Lord loved Israel forever, he has made you king to execute justice and righteousness. (1 Kings 10:9; 2 Chron. 9:8)

Thus says the Lord [to the king of Judah]: Act with justice and righteousness, and deliver from the hand of the oppressor anyone who has been robbed. And do no wrong or violence to the alien, the orphan, and the widow, or shed innocent blood in this place. (Jer. 22:3)

That was the glorious theory. But what about the reality of that royal householding of God's land of Israel? Ever increasing disappointment with royal householders led to ever increasing idealization of David. He was the monarch who became the once and future king in Israel's fervent hope for God's expected messiah-led transformation:

The days are surely coming, says the Lord, when I will raise up for David a righteous Branch, and he shall reign as king and deal wisely, and shall execute justice and righteousness in the land. (Jer. 23:5)

In those days and at that time I will cause a righteous Branch to spring up for David; and he shall execute justice and righteousness in the land. (Jer. 33:15)

That future branch from the ancient Davidic tree, this *anointed* one—*messiah* in Hebrew or *christos* in Greek—is the one celebrated in the magnificent vision of Isaiah 11. But watch the inclusive structure of this accolade:

With *righteousness* he shall judge the poor,
   and decide with equity for the meek of the earth;
he shall strike the earth with the rod of his mouth,
   and with the breath of his lips he shall kill the wicked.

Righteousness shall be the belt around his waist,
    and faithfulness the belt around his loins. (Isa. 11:4–5)

The repetition of "righteousness" frames violence against the wicked of the earth. But that violence is also certainly a mode of *divine rather than human* violence, for this messiah strikes the earth and kills the wicked with mouth and breath alone.

We find the same image in the *Psalms of Solomon,* from the mid-first century BCE. There the "Messiah," the "Son of David," will come "to smash the arrogance of sinners like a potter's jar; to shatter all their substance with an iron rod; to destroy the unlawful nations with the word of his mouth" (17:23–24). There, once again, the messiah acts with divine power.

That raises an obvious question about the Great Divine Cleanup of the World, the eschatological kingdom of God commanded to come in the *Abba* Prayer of Jesus. Is it to be violent or nonviolent? Is it to abolish human violence by divine violence? If so, must God's messianic agent for the Great Cleanup also be violent, armed with the transcendental violence of that avenging God? What, in other words, did Jesus then—and do we now—imagine as the content of "Your kingdom come"?

————

Apart from diverse interpretations of messianic deliverance within this or that Jewish group, there was also a basic, general, and popular expectation of the awaited messiah among ordinary people. He would be the new David, a warrior leader like the old David a thousand years earlier. The new David would militarily liberate his people from their Roman oppressors now, as the old David had delivered them from their Philistine oppressors centuries before. But, now the problem becomes immediately obvious.

On the one hand, all throughout the New Testament—from the first chapter of Matthew (1:1) to the last chapter of Revelation (22:16)—Jesus is proclaimed as the Davidic messiah. On the other

hand, it is equally clear that the historical Jesus was not exactly a warrior prince. Loving your enemies and turning the other cheek are not
military tactics. So how, then, can Jesus be called the Davidic messiah
for those first Messianic or Christian Jews?

Could it be that Jesus himself—and thence his first companions and
later followers—had a different vision of *eschaton,* apocalypse, and messiah? Did their understanding differ from that more popular vision of
the new David as warrior liberator? And, if so, how are we to understand
that distinctive vision in the *Abba* Prayer's "Your *kingdom* come"?

How, for example, did their imagination fill out the details of
that messianic, apocalyptic, and eschatological *kingdom* of God
from Daniel 7? This is not, by the way, a question about how Christianity separated itself from Judaism. It is a question about how one
distinctive Jewish option and group—that of messianic or Christian
Judaism—distinguished itself from other Jewish options and groups
in the Jewish homeland in that fateful first century CE.

My proposal is that Jesus had an interpretation of God's Great
Cleanup of the World that differed radically from the more general
expectation among his own people. You could call his alternative
vision a tradition swerve, a paradigm shift, a model change, or even a
disruptive innovation. My own preference is to describe the challenge
of his kingdom movement—and thence of the "kingdom coming" in
his prayer—as a paradigm-shift within contemporary Judaism.

The term *paradigm shift* was originally used over forty years ago
to explain the transition from an established scientific viewpoint to
a radically new one—for example, from Newtonian to Einsteinian
physics. A standard paradigm, ordinary model, or traditional interpretation continues undisturbed for such a long time that we think
of it as reality itself. Problems, anomalies, and things that do not fit
tend to get swept under the rug of normalcy, until the mound gets so
big that people start stumbling over it. But the set paradigm or nor-
mative model holds fast until a new vision emerges that explains not
only all that the older one did, but also those other discrepancies that
the old model could not.

The term *paradigm shift* is actually useful not just for scientific revolutions, but for many other tradition swerves in human experience—in art and literature, in music and drama, in politics and religion. And, indeed, the first century CE had paradigm shifts in several other crucial areas. By the start of that century Rome was successfully shifting its political paradigm from a republic led by two aristocrats to an empire led by one autocrat. By its end Judaism was successfully shifting its religious paradigm from Temple sacrifices led by priests to Torah study led by sages. In the middle of that century, in between those two momentous model changes in Roman imperialism and Jewish traditionalism, that of Jesus may have seemed at first but a minor Galilean eccentricity. But, eventually, it too would be as world-changing as they were.

If you grant, then, that the kingdom proclaimed by Jesus was a paradigm shift within the popular expectation of his people, what was its precise content? What was different about it? What hope did it leave behind, and what new hope did it shift to? When, for example, Jesus prayed "Your *kingdom* come," what exactly was the precise meaning of that kingdom of God for his tradition swerve or paradigm shift within eschatological, apocalyptic, and messianic Judaism?

———

What is the best way to sharpen the contrast between the popular contemporary expectation of God's Great Cleanup, or the coming of the kingdom, and that proclaimed by Jesus? I think it is by focusing on the difference between John the Baptist and Jesus the Christ.

This is not a cheap exaltation of Jesus over John. Indeed, I am convinced that Jesus learned powerfully from John—learned what to believe, but also what not to believe—especially about God. Furthermore, the execution of one popular prophet, John, may have protected the other one, Jesus, for a given amount of time under Herod Antipas's prudent rule in Galilee.

On the one hand, it is historically certain that Jesus had earlier accepted John's hope for the imminent eschatological intervention of

God. How is that certain? Because John had baptized Jesus into that vision at the Jordan. And how is that certain? Because of the acute embarrassment in the New Testament gospels about Jesus's baptism by John: Mark accepts it (1:9–10), Matthew protests it (3:13–16), Luke hurries it (3:21), and John omits it (1:29–34).

On the other hand, when we hear Jesus's own voice, we detect both strong respect for John and equally clear separation from him. "Truly I tell you," says Jesus, "among those born of women no one has arisen greater than John the Baptist; yet the least in the kingdom of heaven is greater than he" (Matt. 11:11; Luke 7:28). The baptism movement of John was changed into or replaced by the kingdom movement of Jesus.

Furthermore, even those opponents who disliked both John and Jesus equally described them with very different dismissals. They said that John was a mad ascetic and that Jesus was a drunken profligate: "John the Baptist has come eating no bread and drinking no wine, and you say, 'He has a demon'; the Son of Man has come eating and drinking, and you say, 'Look, a glutton and a drunkard, a friend of tax collectors and sinners' " (Luke 7:33–34). In other words, and leaving aside the nasty name-calling, John and Jesus had—eventually—very divergent programs.

I turn therefore to the contrast between John and Jesus to understand the paradigm shift in the latter's understanding of the kingdom of God and, thence, of what he meant by "Your kingdom come" in his *Abba* Prayer.

John the Baptist was an "apocalyptic" eschatologist. His "revelation" was about the imminent advent of God's kingdom and was not about—as it later became in our gospels—the imminent advent of Jesus as God's messiah. But since a future but imminent event is easy enough to proclaim, why did so many accept and follow him?

John believed that only sin held up God's transformative intervention. So he created a great sacramental and penitential renewal of the Exodus. His followers were first brought out into the desert east of the Jordan and were then brought back into the Jewish homeland through that river. As they passed through it, repentance purified their souls just as water washed their bodies. Thereafter, they were received into the promised land as a regenerated people. Then, surely, said John, God would come, any day now. Surely, said John, once a critical mass of purified people were ready, God would have no further excuse for delay.

John's program was very apocalyptic and also very persuasive. When enough people "were baptized by him in the river Jordan, confessing their sins," then God would arrive: "The one who is more powerful than I is coming after me; I am not worthy to stoop down and untie the thong of his sandals. I have baptized you with water; but he will baptize you with the Holy Spirit" (Mark 1:5, 7–8). That, of course, was not originally about the coming of Jesus, but of God.

Furthermore, this imminent God would be very much an avenging presence. Look at John's metaphors:

His winnowing fork is in his hand, and he will clear his threshing floor and will gather his wheat into the granary; but the chaff he will burn with unquenchable fire. (Matt. 3:12)

Even now the ax is lying at the root of the trees; every tree therefore that does not bear good fruit is cut down and thrown into the fire. (Luke 3:9)

You can see how those images fitted the coming of John's avenging God. But you can also see how, once they were transferred to Jesus, the fit was not so good. That is why Luke thought it necessary to soften John's "brood of vipers" language (Matt. 3:7; Luke 3:7) with this addition:

And the crowds asked him, "What then should we do?" In reply he said to them, "Whoever has two coats must share with anyone who has none; and whoever has food must do likewise." Even tax collectors came to be baptized, and they asked him,

"Teacher, what should we do?" He said to them, "Collect no more than the amount prescribed for you." Soldiers also asked him, "And we, what should we do?" He said to them, "Do not extort money from anyone by threats or false accusation, and be satisfied with your wages." (3:10–14)

But John was wrong, terribly, tragically wrong. He announced the immediate advent of an avenging God and what came was the immediate advent of an avenging local ruler. Herod Antipas, the Rome-appointed governor of Galilee, arrested and executed John. *And God did nothing—no intervention and no prevention.* John died in lonely isolation in Antipas's southern fortress of Machaerus, east of the Jordan. *And God did nothing—no intervention and no prevention.*

Jesus watched, Jesus learned, and Jesus changed. He radically reinterpreted. *Eschaton*—what was it to be? *Apocalypse*—when was it to be? And *messiah*—who was it to be? He changed his understanding not only about the kingdom of God, but about the God of the kingdom. When he finally spoke his own vision with his own voice, Jesus differed profoundly from John in proclaiming a paradigm shift within his contemporary Jewish eschatology. I summarize the contrast between John and Jesus in three points.

Imminence or Presence? John said, as we saw above, that God's Great Cleanup of the World was in the future, but imminent. Jesus, on the other hand, said that it was present, already here. These are a few examples of Jesus's announcement of the kingdom's presence rather than its imminence:

"The kingdom of God is not coming with things that can be observed; nor will they say, 'Look, here it is!' or 'There it is!' For, in fact, the kingdom of God is among you." (Luke 17:20–21)

"The law and the prophets were in effect until John came; since then the good news of the kingdom of God is proclaimed, and everyone tries to enter it by force." (Luke 16:16; Matt. 11:12–13)

"If it is by the finger of God that I cast out the demons, then the kingdom of God has come to you." (Luke 11:20; Matt. 12:28)

"Blessed are the eyes that see what you see! For I tell you that many prophets and kings desired to see what you see, but did not see it, and to hear what you hear, but did not hear it." (Luke 10:23b–24; Matt. 13:16–17)

"The wedding guests cannot fast while the bridegroom is with them, can they? As long as they have the bridegroom with them, they cannot fast. The days will come when the bridegroom is taken away from them, and then they will fast on that day." (Mark 2:19–20; Matt. 9:15–16; Luke 5:34–35)

Jesus came to Galilee, proclaiming the good news of God, and saying, "The time is fulfilled, and the kingdom of God has come near; repent, and believe in the good news." (Mark 1:14b–15; Matt. 4:17)

That final example is particularly significant. Notice that Mark does not say that God's kingdom "is coming near" or "is approaching," but "has come near" or "has approached."

Intervention or Collaboration? It is hard, however, to realize how absurd the proclamation of the kingdom's presence must have sounded to its first hearers. Where, they would have asked Jesus, is God's transfigured world to be seen? Is not Tiberius still emperor of Rome, Antipas still tetrarch of Galilee, and Pilate still prefect of Judea? How has anything changed in a world of peasant poverty, local injustice, and imperial oppression?

In answer Jesus proclaimed another—and necessarily concomitant—aspect of his paradigm shift within contemporary eschatological expectation. You have been waiting for God, he said, while God has been waiting for you. No wonder nothing is happening. You want God's intervention, he said, while God wants your collaboration. *God's kingdom is here, but only insofar as you accept it, enter it, live it, and thereby establish it.*

That is why Jesus did not settle down in Nazareth or Capernaum and have his companions bring others to him. Instead, he sent them out to do exactly what he himself was doing: heal the sick, eat with the healed, and demonstrate the kingdom's presence in that reciprocity and mutuality. It is not, he said, about intervention by God, but about participation with God. God's Great Cleanup of the World does not begin, cannot continue, and will not conclude without our divinely empowered participation and transcendentally driven collaboration.

Violence or Nonviolence? As noted above, Jesus did not fit the ordinary paradigm of a new David as warrior deliverer of his people. In other words, the paradigm shift he announced did not imagine himself or others in violent collaboration with a violent God. Neither, of course, did John advocate violent resistance, but his image of a violent God left certain options open.

Jesus, however, gave the nonviolence of God as the reason for his own refusal to resort to violence. The kingdom's presence demanded nonviolent collaboration between the divine and the human—even or especially against violence itself. Recall the reason Jesus gave for nonviolent resistance to evil: "Love your enemies and pray for those who persecute you" (Matt. 5:44); "Love your enemies, do good to those who hate you, bless those who curse you, pray for those who abuse you" (Luke 6:28). But why? "So that you may be children of your Father in heaven; for he makes his sun rise on the evil and on the good, and sends rain on the righteous and on the unrighteous. . . . Be perfect, therefore, as your heavenly Father is perfect" (5:45, 48). Like God, like Jesus, we are called to nonviolent resistance to the violent normalcy of civilization.

The strongest witness to that nonviolent eschatology of Jesus is actually Pilate, the Roman governor who executed him in Jerusalem.

On the one hand, that official publicly, legally, and officially crucified him for *resistance* to Roman law and order. On the other hand, he
made no attempt to round up the disciples of Jesus. He understood—
correctly—that the kingdom movement was one of *nonviolent* resistance. Compare, for example, that story about Barabbas, who "was
in prison with the rebels who had committed murder during the
insurrection" (Mark 15:7). Jesus met the precise fate of public but
nonviolent resistance to Roman law and order. According to the terms
of his imperial mandate, Pilate was precisely correct: public execution
for Jesus, but no communal arrest for his companions.

This was also illustrated powerfully in that parabolic interaction
between Pilate and Jesus in John's gospel. "My kingdom," says Jesus
in 18:36a, "is not of this world" (KJV) or "is not from this world"
(NRSV). We often cite the sentence only up to that point and thereby
make it extremely ambiguous. Does "not from this world" mean we
concern ourselves with future rather than present? Heaven rather than
earth? Religion rather than politics? The interior life rather than the
exterior one?

Jesus continues, however, and makes all those preliminary interpretations irrelevant in 18:36b:

> "If my kingdom were from this world, my followers would be
> fighting to keep me from being handed over to the Jews. But as
> it is, my kingdom is not from here."

I leave aside John's standard prejudice about "the Jews" to emphasize
the structure of those sentences. The repetition of the idea "not from
this world" ("if . . . from this world"—it's not—and "not from here")
frames what cannot and did not happen. The followers of Jesus did
not "fight," did not use violence even to attempt his release.

The difference between God's kingdom and Rome's empire, between
Jesus and Pilate, between Jesus's companions and Pilate's followers is
that *one is nonviolent* and *the other is violent*. Violence cannot be used even
to protect or free Jesus. The coming of God's kingdom, the dawn of es-

chatological transformation, the Great Divine Cleanup of the World—
by whatever name—is nonviolent, and so also are our God-empowered
participation in it and God-driven collaboration with it.

———

There is one final and very important question. What is the connection between the collaborative eschatology of God's kingdom already
present on earth and Christ's future return, second coming, or *parousia*
(Greek for an imperial-level visitation)? Is that latter event the actual
coming of God's kingdom, so that its "presence" on earth before that
moment is merely visionary, preparatory, and promissory? Despite
those sayings cited above, is the kingdom of God about a future with
God in heaven and not about a present with God on earth? Or does
it involve both those aspects—a presence now and a consummation
later?

It is crucially important to distinguish between faith in an imminent *beginning* of God's kingdom and faith in an imminent *end* to that
eschatological kingdom. Saying that something will begin soon is very
different from saying that it has already begun but will end soon. The
former was the Baptist's vision, and it was the normal paradigm for
contemporary Jewish eschatological expectation. But, granted Jesus's
paradigm shift from imminence by divine intervention to presence by
divine-human collaboration, did Jesus also expect an imminent end
to that collaborative vision?

On the one hand, certain sayings *attributed* to Jesus speak of an
imminent consummation: "Truly I tell you, you will not have gone
through all the towns of Israel before the Son of Man comes" (Matt.
10:23); "Truly I tell you, there are some standing here who will not
taste death until they see that the kingdom of God has come with
power" (Mark 9:1). But there are also major scholarly objections to the
notion that those came from the historical Jesus rather than from the
later Jesus tradition.

On the other hand, most of the New Testament authors expected
an imminent conclusion and early consummation to the presence

of God's kingdom on earth. Some scholars have argued that such a general Christian expectation must have derived from Jesus himself. That expectation is very evident from Paul of Tarsus in the early 50s to John of Patmos in the early 90s.

First, Paul expected it within his own lifetime: "*We* who are alive . . . will be caught up in the clouds . . . to meet the Lord in the air" (1 Thess. 4:17); "The appointed time has grown short. . . . For the present form of this world is passing away" (1 Cor. 7:29–31); "Salvation is nearer to *us* now than when we became believers; the night is far gone, the day is near" (Rom. 13:11–12).

Second, John speaks in the book of Revelation about "what must soon take place" (1:1; 22:6), and Jesus himself says repeatedly there, "I am coming soon" (2:16; 3:11; 22:7, 12, 20). John says that Jesus Christ "made us to be a kingdom, priests serving his God and Father, to him be glory and dominion forever and ever" (1:6; 5:10); and that "the kingdom of the world has become the kingdom of our Lord and of his Messiah, and he will reign forever and ever" (11:15; 12:10). So, if God's kingdom has already happened, what is left to happen "soon"?

I myself am convinced that Jesus concentrated on the challenge of God's present but collaborative kingdom, so that his original words and deeds had very little if anything to say about the future—whether near or distant. But *if* he did speak about some immediate consummation of God's kingdom on this earth, we should honestly admit that he—like all those similar New Testament claims—was wrong by about two thousand years—so far. We should not, of course, use that mistake about the future to negate the challenge about the present.

Indeed, it was almost inevitable that the normal concept of the *imminent* start of God's kingdom would reappear after the paradigm shift as the *imminent* end of God's kingdom. It is also almost inevitable that Christians—then and now—prefer to discuss and debate about God's future intervention (or lack of it) than our present collaboration (or lack of it). But, in any case, the *Abba* Prayer's challenge about God's kingdom coming is not about the imminence of divine intervention, but about the empowerment of human collaboration.

Here is what counts: *God's kingdom did not, could not, and will not begin, continue, or conclude without human collaboration.* It will not happen by divine intervention alone—neither to start, continue, or conclude. That is why Matthew's *Abba* Prayer has two even parts with the divine "you" in the first half and the human "we" in the second half. And those two parts are correlatives. They come together or never come at all. They are like two sides of the same eschatological coin. Have you ever seen a one-sided coin?

All of that was precisely summed up by two African bishops who lived at either end of the continent about a millennium and a half apart. "God made you without you," said Augustine of Hippo in 416, "but he doesn't justify you without you." That was magnificently misquoted by Desmond Tutu of Cape Town in 1999: "St. Augustine says, 'God, without us, will not; as we, without God, cannot.'"

I now look backward to prepare for what is to follow. In Chapter 2 we saw that the Lord's Prayer has two balanced halves with three short sections in each half. We also saw that those two halves vibrate together in the traditional poetic parallelism seen so often in the poems and prose poems of the Bible. I also suggested that the divine triplet of name, kingdom, and will and the human triplet of bread, debt, and temptation were like two sides of the same coin.

The challenge of my coin metaphor is that the coin's two sides can be distinguished (say, heads from tails), but not separated. So also with the two sides of the *Abba* Prayer. Furthermore, although we always know that a coin has two sides, we are unable to see them both directly at the same time. (Try it.) There is, in other words, always the danger that we will think only of one *or* the other—only of the "Your" side *or* the "Our" side. The challenge is, of course, always and ever to think dialectically—not of one or the other half of the prayer, but of both together as in responsorial chant.

We are ready now to move, in the next chapter, to the third and final part of the prayer's first half. And here I recognize another parallelism. The final challenge of each half is, I suggest, possibly the most climactically important but definitely the hardest one in each half. We will see that facet of "our" temptation later so I concentrate now on "your" will.

Why is God's will more difficult for us than God's name or God's kingdom? Because "will" is simply such a downright anthropomorphic or flatly human-just-like-us word. Many nonhuman subjects have names and even reputations—what do you think about the Grand Canyon? Many nonhuman subjects have kingdoms—we even have a film and play called *The Lion King*. But "will" seems irrevocably a human-just-like-us word. We move, therefore, onto very difficult theological terrain when we speak of God's will. But it is there as the climax of the *Abba* Prayer's first half and, therefore, we cannot avoid thinking about it.

5

Your Will Be Done on Earth

Thy will be done in earth, as it is in heaven.

Matthew 6:10, KJV

Your will be done, on earth as it is in heaven.

Matthew 6:10, NRSV

On the night between Wednesday and Thursday, November 9 and 10, 1938, Hitler's Nazi government found the excuse it wanted to instigate a controlled public pogrom of German Jews. Earlier that evening, Ernst vom Rath, third secretary at the German embassy in Paris, died of bullet wounds from an assassination by a seventeen-year-old Jewish boy named Herschel Grynszpan.

That night, *Kristallnacht,* or "Night of Shattered Glass," resulted in the murder of 91 Jews, the destruction of over 1,500 synagogues and 7,500 stores and businesses, and the arrest of over 25,000 Jews. It was one more step in the obscene Nazi program that included laws of discrimination, acts of persecution, and extermination camps.

The largest and most beautiful synagogue in all of Germany had stood for one hundred years high above the river Elbe in Dresden, capital city of Prussian Saxony. That November night it was deliberately set on fire by paramilitary brigades who forced the firefighters to let it burn while preventing any spread to adjacent buildings. (Still, one of them, Alfred Neugebauer, saved its Star of David throughout the war until a new synagogue was consecrated on the same location on November 9, 2001.)

On the night between Shrove Tuesday and Ash Wednesday, February 13 and 14, 1945, the first of four Allied air raids deliberately created a perfect firestorm roaring outward from the timbered building of Dresden's Old City center. Hundreds of heavy bombers—Lancasters of the Royal Air Force Bomber Command by night and B-17 Flying Fortresses of the United States Army Air Force by day—used an intentional mix of 60 percent explosive and 40 percent incendiary bombs to ignite the ancient city and raise the heat level to almost half that of an atomic blast.

My present question is not whether there were valid and valuable military targets in Dresden or whether, if present, they were actually targeted. Nor is my present question whether that firestorm was a strategic or tactical, legal or moral action for that date in the war or that place in the conflict. My question arises from the story recorded by Frederick Taylor in his 2004 book, *Dresden: Tuesday, February 13, 1945*. As the synagogue burned on that *Kristallnacht* in 1938,

> a grizzled Dresden street character named Franz Hackel . . . the "Dresden Diogenes" . . . [was] gazing in silent horror at the still-smoking ruins of the Dresden synagogue. He approached the painter [Otto Griebel], his tone conspiratorial, eyes blazing, and muttered: "This fire will return! It will make a long curve and then come back to us!"[1]

I want to think, throughout this chapter, about the internal dynamics of that "long curve" and how the fires of November 1938 begot the fires of February 1945.

I also want to think, throughout this chapter, about another metaphor from geometry. On August 16, 1967, Dr. Martin Luther King Jr. told the Tenth Anniversary Convention of the Southern Christian

Leadership Conference in Atlanta: "The arc of the moral universe is long, but it bends toward justice." Might it even be that the long, slow arc of human history or even human evolution bends toward justice?

What exactly does Hackel's curve or King's arc have to do with God's will? Consider, to begin with, the distinction between *punishments* and *consequences*. I do not equate those terms, as parents often do when they tell their children that "there will be consequences" and mean "there will be punishments." For me, a punishment is an externally added penalty. Example: a drunk driver hits a tree and *is fined* by the police. A consequence is an internally derived result. Example: a drunk driver hits a tree and *is killed* by the impact. Based on that distinction, this chapter begins with a probe into whether God's "will" involves divine punishments or human consequences.

Psalm 82 is quite unusual within the general biblical tradition. It imagines God not as the *only* God, but as the supreme God over all the other Gods, the Powers-That-Be, who administer the world here below. It opens like this:

> God has taken his place in the divine council;
> in the midst of the gods he holds judgment. (82:1)

Why is any "judgment" necessary? Because those whose duty it is to run the world under the supreme God have failed dismally to keep it a just and equitable place. God speaks to them:

> "How long will you judge unjustly
> and show partiality to the wicked?
> Give *justice* to the weak and the orphan;
> maintain the *right* of the lowly and the destitute.
> Rescue the weak and the needy;
> deliver them from the hand of the wicked." (82:2–4)

It is striking, by the way, within the poetic parallelism of those three verses that "justice" is considered a "right" of the defenseless. But it is what comes next that concerns me here. After God reads off that catalogue of cosmic malpractice, the psalm continues:

> They have neither knowledge nor understanding,
>> they walk around in darkness;
>> all the foundations of the earth are shaken. (82:5)

Those three lines are not just in parallelism; they form a crescendo. The indicted rulers do not even make excuses. They do not even recognize their global obligations under the supreme God. "Who said anything about justice?" you can imagine them responding. "Why even bring up this justice thing? Is rule not simply about power?" But watch what happens next.

First, the result is not simply that their malpractice disobeys or disdains the will of the supreme God. The injustice of those rulers shakes the foundations of the earth. That is not a divine punishment, but a human consequence. Second, there isn't even any punishment for those failed rulers. The opening verse promised "judgment," but here is what happens next:

> I say, "You are gods,
>> children of the Most High, all of you;
>> nevertheless, you shall die like mortals,
>> and fall like any prince." (82:6–7)

We were waiting for some sort of punishment, but what did we get? Not punishment, but consequences.

Zeus was a mighty God whose power was carried on the pikes of Alexander's phalanxes from the plains of Macedonia to the mountains of the Hindu Kush. Then one day he died. Nobody killed him. He just became irrelevant. Jupiter too was a mighty God carried on the swords of Rome's legions from the shores of the Irish Sea to the banks of the Euphrates River. Then one day he too died. Again, nobody killed him. He simply became irrelevant. Those were not divine punishments, only human consequences for those failed rulers. Gods of power die when the human power that supports them falters and fails. But how could a God of justice ever die? Would you not first have to destroy the thirst for justice in every human heart?

Genesis 1 tells us we are "images of God," and Paul calls us "heirs of God." Our freedom is to accept or reject that responsibility for God's world. So we should think much less about heavenly punishments and much more about earthly consequences. We humans are, in fact, that "divine council" of Psalm 82. Holding all of that in mind, I turn back to this chapter's subject, to the climactic third challenge in the first half of the Lord's Prayer.

———

You will recall from Chapter 1 that the prayer's earliest versions were not those fuller liturgical ones in Matthew, Luke, or *The Teaching* (see the Appendix). Before them we had the Lord's Prayer concentrated in that bilingual Aramaic and Greek cry of "*Abba,* the Father" in Galatians 4:6, Romans 8:15, and Mark 14:36. Beside that titular address of *Abba* and/or Father, there is one other word that appears in both Romans and Mark connected with the *Abba* Prayer as well as in the Lord's Prayer of Matthew. That common term is the "will of God."

As we already saw in Chapter 1, Paul concludes his great commentary on the *Abba* Prayer in Romans with this:

The Spirit helps us in our weakness; for we do not know how to pray as we ought, but that very Spirit intercedes with sighs too deep for words. And God, who searches the heart, knows what is the mind of the Spirit, because the Spirit intercedes for the saints according to the *will* of God. (8:26–27)

Our collaborative prayer—with the divine Spirit empowering our human spirit—is "according to the will of God" (literally, "according to

God"). But that hardly adds much that is new. God's Spirit is attuned to God's will. Of course. But Mark 14:36 is a very different case.

In Mark, the "will of God" comes up as Jesus prays in agony among those ancient olive trees on the night before his crucifixion:

> They went to a place called Gethsemane; and he said to his disciples, "Sit here while I pray." He took with him Peter and James and John, and began to be distressed and agitated. And he said to them, "I am deeply grieved, even to death; remain here, and keep awake." And going a little farther, he threw himself on the ground and prayed that, if it were possible, the hour might pass from him. He said, "Abba, Father, for you all things are possible; remove this cup from me; yet, not what I will, but what you will." (14:32–36)

How could God "will" the execution of Jesus? And how can Jesus— or anyone else—pray "your will be done" to a God who "wills" such unjust imperial violence?

In Mark a connection between the prayer of Jesus and his execution is seen not only in the address to "*Abba, the Father*" and the mention of God's "will," but also in one other significant link, to be seen more fully in Chapter 8. The prayer concludes with "lead us not into temptation," and Jesus warns Peter in Gethsemane:

> "Simon, are you asleep? Could you not keep awake one hour? Keep awake and pray that you may not enter into temptation; the spirit indeed is willing, but the flesh is weak." (14:37–38)

Whether you translate it "temptation" (KJV) or "time of trial" (NRSV), the Greek word is the same.

I am inclined, therefore, to conclude that Mark may have known a fuller version of the Lord's Prayer, but reserved it for use in the Gethsemane narrative. That made the Lord's Prayer a fervently actual prayer of the Lord. It is even more certain that Luke made that precise transition. And here is why.

One of the major differences between the versions of the *Abba* Prayer in Matthew 6:9–13 and Luke 11:2–4 is that Luke completely omits "Your will be done, on earth as it is in heaven." However, Luke rephrases Mark's Gethsemane prayer of Jesus into this:

> He withdrew from them about a stone's throw, knelt down, and prayed, "Father, if you are willing, remove this cup from me; yet, not my will but yours be done." (Luke 22:41–42)

Luke's Greek has the same noun for God's "will" and the same imperative verb for "be done" as Matthew's version of the *Abba* Prayer does. I conclude that Luke knew that challenge about God's will in the Lord's Prayer, but omitted it in 11:2–4 to hold it over for inclusion on the lips of Jesus himself in 22:42. All of that simply emphasizes my question: Does God will the execution of Jesus and is that at least implicitly included in the Lord's Prayer itself?

———

For millions of Christians the answer to that question has been and still is an emphatic: "Yes, of course, God willed the death of Jesus." The theology that grounds that response was visually portrayed in Mel Gibson's 2004 film *The Passion of the Christ*. That is why it received such enthusiastic approval and financial support from so many Christians.

Their theological interpretation of Christian faith goes like this. Humans sinned against God, but no punishment was adequate to that infinite dishonor. Jesus, however, was both human (like us) and divine (like God). He was therefore the only adequate subject for divine punishment. That understanding is called *vicarious satisfaction* or *substitutionary atonement,* because the sinless Jesus was punished *instead of* or *in the place of* sinful humanity.

I first saw *The Passion of the Christ* during a convention of the Global Pastors Network (GPN) at Calvary Assembly of God Church in downtown Orlando on January 21, 2004, about a month before its public opening. That understanding of the suffering and death of Jesus as vicarious atonement for human sin was already evident in the film's promotional advertising, especially posters with the line: "Dying Was His Reason for Living." That was also why the film explicitly focused on the last twelve hours of the life of Jesus and why the resurrection became irrelevant. That theology of Jesus as replacement victim was all about dying and not about either living beforehand or rising afterward.

After the screening, Mel Gibson was interviewed onstage by Dr. James O. Davis, one of the founders of the GPN. Mr. Gibson said that Jesus had to bear the punishment for all human sin since the dawn of creation and that, even though Jesus could have atoned for that with one drop of blood from his pricked finger, he chose to accept the fullest measure of suffering due for such cosmic evil. In that theology, God's "will" certainly included and indeed demanded the execution of Jesus. But when did that theology begin? It is certainly not present in the New Testament itself.

Jesus spoke of *collaboration,* not substitution. When he warned his companions about his fateful journey to Jerusalem, he did not say that he went *instead of* them. He said: "If any want to become my followers, let them deny themselves and take up their cross and follow me" (Mark 8:34). That is collaboration, not substitution.

Paul, likewise, spoke of *participation,* not substitution. "In Christ" is his favorite expression, never "by Christ." Or think of this rhapsodic acclamation: "All of us, with unveiled faces, seeing the glory of the Lord as though reflected in a mirror, are being transformed into the same image from one degree of glory to another; for this comes from the Lord, the Spirit" (2 Cor. 3:18). That, once again, is about our participation with Jesus and not our replacement by Jesus.

I repeat my question. When, why, how, and where did that theology of *substitution* arise? The answer to the "when" part is: not until a thousand years after the time of Jesus. It arose only at the very end of Christianity's first millennium. But why, how, and where?

———

In April 1098, Otho de Lagery and Anselmo d'Aosta, two of Western Christianity's most important clerics, met at the Vatican in Rome. They were in their sixties and deeply involved in opposing projects. Both projects would be profoundly important for politics and religion right down to our present day. And both projects would be—each in its own way—profoundly disastrous.

Otho de Lagery is better known as Pope Urban II. In November 1095, at the Council of Clermont in south-central France, he gave a lurid description of what Muslims were doing to Christians in Jerusalem. "Enter upon the road to the Holy Sepulchre," he said (as a scribe known as Peter the Monk recorded later), "wrest that land from the wicked race, and subject it to yourselves." The result was that all cried out in miraculous unison: "It is the will of God! It is the will of God!"

The "First Crusade" is what we now call what followed. It started with the persecution of Western Jews and ended with the slaughter of Eastern Muslims. Jerusalem fell in the middle of July 1099, and Urban II died about two weeks later. That was one vision of God's "will."

Anselmo d'Aosta became archbishop of Canterbury in 1093. Philosopher and theologian, monk and bishop, mystic and saint, Anselm preferred nonviolent debate to violent crusade. His idea was to defend the incarnation and crucifixion of Jesus by confronting those he called "infidels"—that is, Jews and Muslims—with reason and logic alone. He started his book *Why Did God Become a Human Being?* (in Latin, *Cur Deus Homo?*) in 1095 while still in England. That, by the way, was the same year that the seeds of the First Crusade were planted when the Byzantine emperor begged Urban II for assistance against the Muslim Turks threatening Constantinople from as near as Nicea. Anselm finished his book in 1098 after that visit to Rome, but while still in Italy under royal exile from England.

His purpose, as he tells us in the book's prologue, was to argue against "infidels, who despise the Christian faith because they deem it contrary to reason." To do so he would leave "Christ out of view (as if nothing had ever been known of him)" and prove "by absolute reasons" and "plain reasoning" that both the incarnation and crucifixion of Christ were necessary, so that all may "enjoy a happy immortality, both in body and in soul."

It is from Anselm's book that we got that argument for *vicarious satisfaction* or *substitutionary atonement* outlined above. Again and again throughout his presentation, Anselm mentions the "will of God." Here are just a few examples:

It is then plain that no one can honor or dishonor God, as he is in himself; but the creature, as far as he is concerned, appears to do this when he submits or opposes his will to the *will of God*. (1.15)

So heinous is our sin whenever we knowingly oppose the *will of God* even in the slightest thing; since we are always in his sight, and he always enjoins it upon us not to sin. (1.21)

Since, then, the *will of God* does nothing by any necessity, but of his own power, and the will of that man [Christ] was the same as the will of God, he died not necessarily, but only of his own power. (2.17)

Anselm is quite clear on why God must "will" the incarnation and crucifixion of Jesus and why God cannot simply forgive everyone without any punishment at all. That would mean, he says, that God is indifferent to evil, that God does not care about sin one way or another. But that would be impossible, he concludes, for a just God. God must therefore "will" adequate punishment for human sin, and only the both human and divine Jesus is an appropriate victim.

Anselm's logic is flawless, and that is probably why his theology is so persuasive. But that flawless logic depends on two presuppositions. The first one takes us back to Chapter 2 and the importance of metaphor, especially of those basic ones we need when speaking of God. What is the dominant metaphor guiding Anselm's vision of God and presumed every time he argues—quite logically—about the will of that God?

When I was growing up in Ireland in the late 1940s, two eleventh-century battles and their dates were pounded into our young heads. One was the Battle of Clontarf in 1014. For over a century before that date, Viking raiders—superb sailors from Scandinavia—came down the North Atlantic and up the Irish rivers in their wide but shallow-draught longboats. They plundered monasteries, established trading towns, and were finally defeated at Clontarf just north of Dublin on Good Friday in April 1014.

The other was the Battle of Hastings in 1066. Vikings had settled down in northern France as "Norsemen" or "Normans," with walled castles and armored cavalry instead of those fighting longboats. In October 1066 they successfully invaded England under William I the Conqueror, and about one hundred years later they had moved westward across the Irish Sea. The Vikings, in other words, eventually conquered Ireland.

This is the context that gave Anselm his metaphor. He was the second *Norman* archbishop of the conquered Anglo-Saxons. He had been appointed, in fact, by the second *Norman* ruler, William II Rufus, in March 1093. It was actually two years before the pope's official approval arrived. Norman kings were feudal lords whose identity, honor, and integrity demanded that just retribution be administered for all offenses. Indeed, the security and stability of their Norman empire—especially in newly conquered England—demanded that procedure. Feudal lords were like, say, our judges in courts of law; they could not walk into the room and forgive everyone in sight. God, for Anselm, was the *Norman*-style Lord of the Universe. Forgiveness of evil would have meant indifference to evil.

What, however, if you change that foundational metaphor on which the logic of vicarious punishment totally depends? What if you imagine God not as a transcendental *Norman Lord,* but as a transcendental *Jewish Householder?* The Lord's Prayer did not begin, after all, with: "Our Judge, who art in Court," but with "Our Father, who art in heaven." What would the image of Father as Householder do to Anselm's powerful logic?

There is also another presupposition behind Anselm's logic. His major argument was that God had to punish evil or else he was not a just God. At a first hearing, that seems absolutely correct:

> It is not proper for God to pass over sin unpunished. . . . It is not fitting that God should take sinful man without an atonement. . . . This cannot be effected unless satisfaction be made, which none but God can make and none but man ought to make, [so] it is necessary for the God-man to make it. (*Cur Deus Homo?* 1.12, 19; 2.6)

But what if God's justice and righteousness operate not by punishments, but by consequences? And what, then, if the focus of divine justice and the interpretation of God's will were removed from externally added *punishments* and placed on internally derived *consequences?*

My own proposal is that, from the divine creation in Genesis 1, through the divine council in Psalm 82, and on to Hackel's curve and King's arc, the equitable distribution of our world is a necessity built into the very destiny of that world. We do not, it seems, get away with injustice for very long.

I have profound respect for Anselm as a monk and a saint. He could easily have been martyred under William II by the end of the eleventh century. That happened to Thomas Becket, another archbishop of Canterbury, under Henry II by the end of the next century. With William and Anselm, the clash between English king and Roman pope was already heading for its consummation under Henry VIII in the sixteenth century.

But, although I know that our mega-metaphors for God are always conditioned by time and place, here is what I cannot understand. Anselm was a monk for forty-nine years and an archbishop for only sixteen years. Even within patriarchal parameters, then, why not imagine God as a monastic abbot rather than a feudal lord or as a spiritual director rather than a Norman king? Monasteries were, as Anselm well understood, places for slow transformation and not for swift punishment. "How sad," said Sophocles a millennium and a half earlier in his play *Antigone,* "when those who reason, reason wrong."

———

I have focused discussion of God's will on Urban and Anselm in those waning years of Christianity's first millennium. On the one hand, millions of Christians *probably* agree that the First Crusade and all those succeeding ones were not the will of God. On the other hand, millions of Christians *certainly* consider the passion (from the Latin *passio,* suffering) and death of Jesus to have been the eternal will of God. They would probably argue that Anselm did no more than brilliantly confirm from reason what was already clearly present from revelation in the New Testament itself. They would deny my claim that vicarious atonement was not present there, but was created much later by Anselm himself. They could easily quote texts like these:

God put forward [Christ] as a sacrifice of *atonement* by his blood, effective through faith. He did this to show his righteousness, because in his divine forbearance he had passed over the sins previously committed. (Rom. 3:25)

He [Christ] had to become like his brothers and sisters in every respect, so that he might be a merciful and faithful high priest in the service of God, to make a sacrifice of *atonement* for the sins of the people. (Heb. 2:17)

Those texts raise additional questions about God's will and Jesus's death. Does the biblical tradition of sacrifice, sin, and atonement involve *vicarious* atonement? If you speak of Christ's sacrifice, or sacrifice for sin, or sacrifice for sin as atonement, does any or all of that entail the theme of *substitution*—of Jesus suffering and dying instead of us and in our place? Is *sacrifice,* which is certainly mentioned throughout the Christian Bible, about *substitution*?

To find an answer, I begin with some even wider questions. Why did religions—across time and place—come up with blood sacrifice? Why did religions—independently and cross-culturally—decide that God or the Gods wanted dead animals or dead people?

———

We humans maintain good relations with one another or restore them, if broken, either by a gift or by a meal. That is Anthropology 101. We do exactly the same to make or restore good relations with God or the Gods.

The English word "sacrifice" comes from the Latin *sacrum facere,* "to make sacred." Religions offer gifts or share meals with God or the Gods—that is, they *make* gifts or meals *sacred*—either as request for the future or as gratitude for the past. (Remember those psalm prayers of request and gratitude in Chapter 1.)

In the Jewish tradition, for example, a valuable animal could be offered to God as a gift. It was totally consumed by fire and thus "made sacred" as a holocaust. Alternatively, the animal could be offered to God and then returned to the offerers after having been "made sacred." They could then feast on holy food with their God.

Sacrifice, and especially blood sacrifice, is never about substitution, but always about a gift or meal. But how does that general understanding of blood sacrifice apply to martyrs in general and, thence, to Jesus the Christ in particular?

If you live by demanding justice in an unjust world, there is always the danger of marginalization or discrimination, if not assassination or execution. Martyrs are those who have died for justice or from injustice and have made their lives sacred by such a death. Recall that sacrifice (*sacrum facere*) means to make sacred. We need that word for martyrs—before, with, and after Jesus—who accepted death to retain the integrity of their lives. Such a death is not substitution, but a gift—a supreme gift—to cause or vision, to country or humanity, to God or the Gods.

Furthermore, and apart from the more exceptional case of martyrs, we need that term "sacrifice" for all those who give their lives for others. For example, late in the afternoon of Wednesday, January 13, 1982, Air Florida flight 90 took off from Washington National Airport and almost immediately plunged into the icy Potomac off the 14th Street Bridge. Of the seventy-nine people on board that Boeing 737 only six managed to escape onto the tail as it stuck up above the surface of the river. The rescue helicopter repeatedly dropped lines to them. Arland D. Williams Jr. repeatedly passed the lines to others and, by the time five were saved, he had slipped under the water from hypothermia.

He was the only passenger who died from drowning, and the only adequate headline for his death would not have been "Man Drowns," but "Man Sacrifices His Life." All human life, and all human death, is sacred, but, by giving up his life for others, he had made it specially, emphatically, and particularly sacred, and "to make sacred" is "to sacrifice." He risked, and unfortunately lost, his life *to save others*, but gift, not substitution, is the proper interpretation of his action.

Jesus died to maintain the integrity of his life. Or, to reverse Mel Gibson's claim in *The Passion of the Christ*, "Living Was His Reason for Dying." His nonviolent resistance to violence as a revelation of God's own character was consummated by that execution. We have no word for the crucifixion of Christ other than "sacrifice," a making sacred of both life and death, a gift both to divinity and to humanity. It was never, ever, a substitution for anything. But, still, what about that sacrificial death *for sin* and *as atonement*? How does that fit into Jesus's death and God's will?

I begin, once again, with questions. If you hear the plural word "sins," what comes immediately to your mind? Do you have a list and do you have priorities in it? If you hear the singular word "sin," what are you imagining? Is there—for you—one "sin" that is primary among all others or even summary for all others? Finally, do you know where the word "sin"—in the singular—first appears in the Bible? By whom was it first mentioned? In what context did it first appear?

In answer, I take you back to Chapter 4 and its description of the Neolithic Revolution. We go back to that fateful dawn of civilization on the great plains around the Tigris and Euphrates Rivers. The Sumerians of southern Mesopotamia were the first people we know who created irrigated agriculture, who thought about what was happening to them, and, having invented writing, were able to pass their thoughts down to us today.

They did so by trash-talk debate—yes, they invented that too—between, for example, summer work and winter work, between cattle and grain, between pickax and plow, and between the shepherd god and the farmer god. In the Sumerian story those divine brothers were finally able to reconcile their differences by sharing the water needed for both herding and farming. So, about six thousand years ago it was possible that, as Rodgers and Hammerstein said in *Oklahoma,* "the farmer and the cowman should be friends."

That is not, however, how the Bible records its own version of that same Neolithic Revolution and its dispute between ancient nomadic herding and newly invented irrigated farming. The fascinating biblical *parable* of Genesis 4 details what first happened when humans left the secure precincts of the Garden of Eden and emerged out onto those baked Mesopotamian plains, that "cradle of civilization" now known as Iraq.

First, says Genesis 4, the farmer Cain killed the herder Abel. The opening sin of human history, the beginning of an escalatory process undergirding human history, was the violence of fratricidal murder. Or as God said to Cain: "Sin is lurking at the door; its desire is for you, but you must master it" (4:7). That is, of course, the first mention of "sin" in the Bible, and it is in the singular.

Next, we expect some form of divine penalty. Maybe God will now invent capital punishment and execute Cain for his murder of Abel? But here is what we get:

> The Lord said, "What have you done? Listen; your brother's blood is crying out to me from the ground! And now you are cursed from the ground, which has opened its mouth to receive your brother's blood from your hand. When you till the ground, it will no longer yield to you its strength; you will be a fugitive and a wanderer on the earth." Cain said to the Lord, "My punishment is greater than I can bear!" (4:10–13)

The earth is a living being, and Cain has defiled and desecrated it by shedding murdered human blood upon it. The result is the earth's revulsion, as it were, so that Cain is "cursed" from—or by—the earth itself. Is that human consequence or divine punishment?

Then comes the first city: "Cain knew his wife, and she conceived and bore Enoch; and he [Cain] built a city, and named it Enoch after his son Enoch" (4:17). And, as we now know, if the farmer dooms the herder, the city dooms the farmer. But that would take a long time.

Finally, there is an exponential growth in murderous violence throughout that chapter. In the first stage, Cain kills Abel, and God acknowledges, "Your brother's blood is crying out to me from the ground" (4:10). But there is no violent punishment from God. In the next stage, God warns of the inevitable escalation of the tribal blood feud: "Whoever kills Cain will suffer a sevenfold vengeance" (4:15). In the final stage, the blood feud reaches epidemic proportions. Five generations after Cain, his descendant Lamech boasts:

> "I have killed a man for wounding me,
> a young man for striking me.

If Cain is avenged sevenfold,
    truly Lamech seventy-sevenfold." (4:23–24)

My tribe, says Lamech, will take exponentially escalating vengeance
for my murder. I take very, very seriously that the Bible's first mention
of "sin" is not just fratricidal murder, but *escalatory* violence itself.

Escalatory violence means that we have never invented a weapon we
did not use, never invented one that was not surpassed by the next
one, and never slowed down the speed of that replacement. We got,
for example, from the first iron sword to the first hydrogen bomb in
less than three thousand years.

The death of the nonviolent Jesus as the revelation of God's nonviolent character is a sacrifice (a making sacred) that atones for our sin
of escalatory violence. Furthermore, as Paul insists so repeatedly, all
Christians are called to reject "that world" that rejected Jesus. We are
baptismally committed to resist nonviolently the normal violence with
which "the rulers of this age . . . crucified the Lord of glory" (1 Cor.
2:8). Not just the Romans, but every government our world has ever
known would have removed or silenced Jesus *one way or another*. Those
who demand justice nonviolently are sometimes silenced by injustice
violently. Public execution is simply the older and cruder method.

God did not "will" the death of Jesus as a vicarious *punishment* for
the human sin of escalatory violence. But did God "will" it as a *consequence* for that sin? The execution of Jesus was certainly a consequence
of normal imperial violence and a witness against it on behalf of God.
So did or did not God will it? In answer, we need another distinction
beyond that of externally added punishment or internally derived
consequence.

If we decide to use anthropomorphic, or human-just-like-us, language for God, we should at least allow the same distinctions for
God that we make for ourselves. Parents or householders, for example,
may will something directly, deliberately, or emphatically for their
children. They may also will some other things reluctantly. They may
tolerate them, accept them, allow them, but positively not want them

for those same children. There are, in other words, consequences of freedom that must be accepted even if never willed. So also with what God "wills." Every martyr needs a murderer and God's will allows such events as the positive and negative results of human freedom. God "wills" our human freedom. All else is consequence.

———

My guiding proposal for the *Abba* Prayer as hymnic prose poem is that there is an equal or synonymous poetic parallelism between the first half, about God's name, kingdom, will, and the second half, about our bread, debt, and temptation. They are, in other words, two different ways of describing the same reality, but with, of course, vibrations of difference between them. Furthermore, each half is itself in crescendo or climactic parallelism building up through the three component challenges. "Bread" and "debt" come to a climax in "temptation"—but that will be seen later.

"Name" and "kingdom" come to a climax in "will"—and I turn to that now. Here it is in summary: God's *name* is God's reputation for justice and righteousness. That reputation is established by the advent of God's *kingdom*. That advent was the *will* of God—from all eternity. But where did I get that climactic "eternity"?

As we saw before, the prayer's first half ended with "as in heaven so on earth" in the Greek sequence of Matthew. That "as in heaven" pointed backward to the entire first triad, name, kingdom, and will, just as "so on earth" points forward to the next triad, bread, debt, and temptation. I focus now on "as in heaven." What does it mean?

On the one hand, it simply means that heaven is in great shape—earth is where the problems are. It's God's earthly household, not God's heavenly household, that is in disarray. On the other hand, it means something far more profound.

Think of this question about the collaborative *eschaton,* the kingdom of God, or the Great Divine Cleanup of the World. Did God have a bright new idea, come up with a paradigm shift in divine vision, with the conception of Jesus around 4 BCE?

Some prophetic Jewish mystics peered *across time and into the future* to learn about God's coming kingdom—recall the nighttime dream vision of Daniel 7 in Chapter 4. But others were swept ecstatically *across space and into heaven* to see that divine plan for God's coming kingdom.

Recall that metaphor for God as creation's Architect from Chapter 3. That divine Architect had, as it were, a complete model of the kingdom prepared in heaven above and ready for descent below. It was like seeing the future in an architect's office. So God could reveal the future kingdom not only to seers in a visionary message, but to mystics on a heavenly journey. Furthermore, that master model had been there from all eternity—waiting, waiting, waiting.

Take Paul, for instance. He admitted, with oblique but quite definite reference to himself:

> I know a person in Christ who fourteen years ago was caught up to the third heaven—whether in the body or out of the body I do not know; God knows. And I know that such a person— whether in the body or out of the body I do not know; God knows—was caught up into Paradise and heard things that are not to be told, that no mortal is permitted to repeat. (2 Cor. 12:2–4)

When you hear the "will of God is done in heaven," think not just about angelic obedience; think of the eternal design of God for creation laid out there for any visiting mystic to see. God's name, kingdom, and will come to their climax "in heaven," that is, in their eternal intention.

The metaphor I have in mind for this is a great river pushing relentlessly against a logjam. It was always there pushing, but one day it finally broke through. If we could assess all the variables of time and place, we could possibly explain why it happened at that time and in that way; but barring that, the exact reason for time and place may elude us. "As in heaven" reminds us that God's will for creation was always there and ever the same, but that a window of opportunity opened in the first century CE and "as in heaven" became "so on earth." That is what John says most accurately and poetically at the start of his gospel:

> In the beginning was the Word,
>   and the Word was with God,
>   and the Word was God.
>   He was in the beginning with God. . . .
> And the Word became flesh
>   and lived among us,
>   and we have seen his glory, the glory as of a father's only son,
>   full of grace and truth.
>   From his fullness we have all received, grace upon grace. (1:1–2,
>   11–16)

The Word (*Logos* in Greek) is the eternal vision and creative dream of God for the world. It is the "will" of God for justice and righteousness, which "became flesh" in Jesus of Nazareth.

We are now ready to begin the transition from the former to the latter half of the *Abba* Prayer, from "heaven" to "earth," and so from Chapters 3–5 into Chapters 6–8 of this book. And, at this point, one possible confusion must be mentioned. Are we perhaps not supposed to think about earth in the present, but about heaven in the future?

Possible—and often actual—confusion comes especially from Matthew's language. Although Matthew speaks five times of the "kingdom of God," he speaks thirty-one times about the "kingdom of heaven." Does that latter phrase push God's kingdom into future time in heaven above? Not at all, because Matthew means exactly the same reality by both expressions. Just compare these two verses:

Jesus said to his disciples, "Truly I tell you, it will be hard for a rich person to enter the *kingdom of heaven*. Again I tell you, it is easier for a camel to go through the eye of a needle than for someone who is rich to enter the *kingdom of God.*" (19:23–24)

Matthew respectfully avoids the name of God by using, as it were, the dwelling for the dweller, just as, *mutatis mutandis,* we do by announcing, "The White House says . . . ," when we mean "The President says . . ." For Matthew, "kingdom of heaven" means exactly the same as "kingdom of God." God's kingdom is not about future heaven, but present earth. That is quite clear from the "on earth" in the Lord's Prayer.

It is, indeed, even clearer in the original Greek, "as in heaven so in earth," than in our English translation, "on earth as in heaven." The Greek emphasizes that heaven is where the eternal model exists for our earth, not where the future destiny of our earth awaits.

When "heaven" comes down to "earth," how is our world transformed? What is heaven's process, project, or program for our earth? That is what is outlined with the "bread," "debt," and "temptation" in the parallel second half of the *Abba* Prayer, and I now turn to explore that vision's opening focus on "bread."

6

Give Us Our Daily Bread

Give us this day our daily bread.

Matthew 6:11, KJV, NRSV

It was called the "excavation from hell," because, when first discovered, the first-century Kinneret Boat was the consistency of soft cheese or wet cardboard. And its necessarily swift excavation was followed by a longer and slower, but equally difficult preservation process.

Lake Kinneret is a harp-shaped body of water known to Mark as the "Sea of Galilee" (1:16; 7:31), to John as the "Sea of Galilee, also called the Sea of Tiberias" (6:1), and to Luke, proud of his experience of the Mediterranean Sea, as simply the "lake of Gennesaret" (5:1). But, after the droughts of 1985–86, water levels were so low in the Kinneret that wide swaths of the lake bottom were visible off Magdala on the western shore. And equally visible, almost a mile north of Mary's ancient home, was the oval outline of a sunken boat.

On Friday, January 24, 1986, Moshele and Luvi Lufan, brothers from nearby Kibbutz Ginosar, discovered and protected that mud-embedded boat until official archaeologists arrived—Kurt Raveh and Shelley Wachsmann, from the Israel Antiquities Authority, but especially Orna Cohen, of the Conservation Laboratory at the Hebrew University's Archaeology Institute in Jerusalem. They worked swiftly but extremely carefully to encase the sodden hull in a cocoon of polyurethane, fiberglass, and polyester, which enabled them to float it—yes, actually float it—to Kibbutz Ginosar's recently constructed Yigal Allon Museum. There a crane lifted it onto dry land and, eight days later, into a specially constructed preservation tank.

The boat's timbers were about 90 percent water, which had to be slowly and carefully replaced with polyethylene glycol—the required forty tons were a gift from Dow Chemical. Fourteen years later "The Ancient Galilee Boat"—as the sign says—was finally lifted into its present display position on a stainless-steel frame in the Yigal Allon Centre on the shore of Lake Kinneret.

The 8-by-26-foot boat required a minimum crew of five and could hold either ten passengers or their equivalent weight in cargo. It had four oars, a double rudder, and a square sail. It was, in fact, exactly like a boat on a mosaic excavated earlier in Magdala itself. The keel was one-third cedar—from an older boat; the other two-thirds were carob and jujube (Christ's Thorn). The planks were of cedar and the frames of oak, but, in all, there were twelve different types of wood in the boat.

In other words, it had been kept afloat by expert boatwrights working with inferior materials. Then, one day when even that was no longer possible, they stripped it of everything usable and pushed it out from their boatyard to sink in an offshore graveyard for old boats.

It is but a single boat, but it is also the only one from the first century CE ever discovered in Lake Kinneret. I take it as a symbol—not an argument, let alone a proof—of what life was like on the lake in the time of Jesus. "The Galilee at this time was economically depressed," writes Shelley Wachsmann in his book *The Sea of Galilee Boat.* "The timbers used in the boat's construction are perhaps a physical expression of this overall economic situation."[1] And the late J. Richard Steffy, one of the founding members of the Institute of Nautical Archaeology at Texas A&M University, noting the combination of the boatwrights' excellent craft with inadequate materials, told Wachsmann, "There is something pathetic about this hull."[2] One wonders, of course, for whom and by whom the lake was "economically depressed." One wonders if all, or only some, of the first-century boats on that lake were in such a "pathetic" state.

The Yigal Allon Centre's display of "The Ancient Galilee Boat" is visually beautiful and pedagogically excellent. The wall is dominated by a banner headline in Hebrew and English: "The Mystery of the 2000-Year-Old Boat." Underneath is a giant olive green question mark as big as the lines of questions in Hebrew to its right and in English to its left. Here is how those questions appear (my numbers):

To whom did this boat belong?
[1] To Jesus and his disciples
[2] To the fighters of the Migdal battle
[3] To a fisherman from the Sea of Galilee

Almost the same heading, with "mystery" enlarged, and those same three questions are repeated again in an explanatory placard elsewhere in the room (my numbers):

MYSTERY shrouds the 2000 Year Old Boat
[1] Did this boat witness the events sweeping over the Sea of Galilee in Jesus' time? Is this the boat that bore the Nazarene and his disciples to the surrounding villages to preach the gospel to the people?
[2] Perhaps this was an ordinary fisherman's craft, which was converted for use in battle in the great first-century Jewish rebellion against the Romans.
[3] Or was it a simple fishing boat that plied the waters in quest of the daily catch until it was scuttled and abandoned on the shore?

The simplest answers to those three questions are, respectively, *possibly, probably,* and *certainly.* But what is also certain is that its "crazy-quilt patchwork construction" illustrates the difficult life of at least one peasant fisherman's family on that first-century Sea of Galilee. With that firmly in mind, here are my own three rather different questions.

A First Question. Herod the Great, the Rome-appointed "King of the Jews," died in 4 BCE. The emperor Augustus divided Herod's kingdom among his three sons—Archelaus, Antipas, and Philip. Herod Antipas received Galilee and Perea, two unconnected territories with Galilee to the west and Perea to the east of the upper Jordan. Then, for the next twenty-five years Antipas stayed very quiet, until the 20s CE, when popular unrest against him began. So here is the problem. What did Antipas do differently in the 20s CE to cause animosity after that long and peaceful period?

A *Second Question.* Or, better, the other side of that first question. Why did two successive movements of nonviolent resistance arise in the territories of Antipas in the 20s CE? Remember the baptism movement of John and the kingdom movement of Jesus seen already in Chapter 4. Why, with John in Perea and Jesus in Galilee, did those populist movements start precisely at that time and in that place? Why then? Why there?

A *Third Question.* This one has multiple subquestions. Why is there so much "fishy" stuff in the gospels? Since Jesus was from inland Nazareth, why was it that "he left Nazareth and made his home in Capernaum by the sea [of Galilee]" (Matt. 4:13)? Why were so many of his disciples from fishing villages and specifically from ones on the northwest quadrant of the lake? Think about just these six examples.

Mary was from Magdala, whose Greek name, Tarichaeae, means "salted fish." *Peter* moved from one fishing village, Bethsaida, to live with his wife and mother-in-law at another such village, Capernaum (John 1:44; Mark 1:29–30). Also, *"Philip* was from Bethsaida, the city of *Andrew* and Peter" (John 1:44). And "As Jesus passed along the Sea of Galilee, he saw Simon and his brother Andrew casting a net into the sea—for they were fishermen. . . . As he went a little farther, he saw *James* son of Zebedee and his brother *John,* who were in their boat mending the nets" (Mark 1:16–19). They were called to "fish for people" (Mark 1:17).

Finally, recall all those stories about fish or fishing. There are six versions of the miraculous multiplication of loaves and fishes—two in Mark (6:34–44; 8:1–9), two in Matthew (14:14–21; 15:32–39), and one each in Luke (9:12–17) and John (6:4–13). There is also the story of the net-breaking catch of fish told before the resurrection in Luke 5:1–9 and after it in John 21:1–14.

Jesus is seldom far from boats and nets, fish and fishers, seldom far from the Sea of Galilee, which became the Sea of Tiberias. Why is that, and what does it mean? And, for our present context, what does it have to do with "Give us this day our daily bread"? The *Abba* Prayer is about daily bread, not daily fish. Why so much emphasis on "fish"?

———

Jesus called Herod Antipas "that fox" (Luke 13:32), but although "that fox" planned carefully and moved slowly, he ultimately failed dismally. Throughout forty-three years of rule under three different Roman emperors, he had one driving ambition: to become like his father, Herod the Great, the Rome-appointed "King of the Jews."

Antipas's first attempt brought him before the emperor Augustus at Rome in 4 BCE. His father had first proposed him as his royal heir, but then changed that designation to his brother Archelaus. Augustus gave neither of them the supreme title of "monarch" (full ruler), but made Archelaus "ethnarch" ("people ruler") of Idumea, Judea, and Samaria and Antipas "tetrarch" ("quarter ruler") of (unconnected) Galilee and Perea.

Antipas's third attempt brought him before the emperor Caligula at Rome in 39 CE. But another Herodian prince named Agrippa had grown up at the imperial court and knew well both Caligula and the next emperor, Claudius. Caligula's response to Antipas's request for kingship was to send him into exile, and a few years later it was Agrippa I and not Antipas who became the second and final "King of the Jews."

Antipas's second and main attempt, however, was under Tiberius, the emperor in 14–37 CE, and that is my present focus. Any hope of royal ascendancy required Antipas to succeed on two fronts simultaneously. Externally, for his Roman masters, he had to increase his productivity and, internally, for his Jewish subjects, he had to increase his popularity. He could fail on one front if the Galilean peasantry rebelled against him at home and on the other if the Jerusalem aristocracy appealed against him at Rome.

As he moved cautiously forward on both fronts, Antipas modeled his actions on those of Herod the Great. His father had curried imperial Roman favor by building a new capital city and a magnificent state-of-the-art port at Caesarea on the coast. He had also garnered popular support with a very political marriage.

A Jewish royal family known as the Hasmoneans had ruled a then independent Jewish homeland for one hundred years before the Romans arrived in the 60s BCE. When the Romans conquered the land of Israel, they replaced the Hasmonean with the Herodian dynasty. Then, in the hope of appeasing the people and decreasing general resentment, Herod the Great married a Hasmonean princess named Mariamne. But Herod the Great, who often makes Henry VIII look both magnanimous and monogamous, eventually executed his Hasmonean queen.

Herod Antipas got his model for imperial advancement from his dead father. He planned a new capital city for increased productivity and a new political marriage for increased popularity.

Productivity. Sepphoris, Antipas's first capital city, looked out from its centrally located hillock onto the surrounding valleys and hillsides fertile with cereals, olives, and grapes. Not much more could be done there to increase his tax base from peasants living mainly at subsistence level and always in danger of slipping downward from small landowners to tenant farmers to day laborers.

His solution was to create a new capital city, to locate it on the mid-western shore of the Sea of Galilee, and to name it Tiberias in honor of the new emperor. For reasons religious and political, social and economic, capital cities tended to stay where they were—apart, that is, from natural disasters rendering them uninhabitable. So, granted Antipas wanted a capital city, why put it at that location? Why on the lake? What was Antipas's intention for Tiberias when it finally opened for business at the start of the 20s CE?

It was, quite simply, to commercialize the Sea of Galilee and make it, as we saw above, the Sea *of Tiberias*. Romanization worked by urbanization for commercialization, and Antipas planned to exploit the lake the way he was already exploiting the land. Think about exports: dried fish, salted fish, and even that execrable fish sauce, called *garum*, that the Romans loved so well.

Popularity. To guarantee his general popularity across the entire country, Antipas decided on his own version of a Hasmonean-Herodian connection. He divorced his wife, a princess from Arab Nabatea in Transjordan. And he persuaded Herodias, granddaughter of the beloved Mariamne, to divorce her husband, Herod (Philip?). Double divorce and, of course, double trouble.

You can now understand how both John and Jesus deliberately undermined that drive for increased popularity and how intolerable such opposition to their hopeful plans must have been for Herodias and Antipas. John the Baptist told Antipas, "It is not lawful for you to have your brother's wife" (Mark 6:18); and Jesus told them both, "Whoever divorces his wife and marries another commits adultery against her; and if she divorces her husband and marries another, she commits adultery" (Mark 10:11–12). Those accusations were not just moral criticism, but political interference with Antipas's royal plans.

Imagine as well what his plans for Tiberias did to peasant fishers and their villages along the lake. There were probably taxes for every stage of fishing—for having a boat, for fishing with dragnets, maybe even for casting a net from the shore. You might also have to sell your catch to Antipas's warehouses for dried and salted fish. No wonder Jesus's two most prominent disciples—Mary and Peter—were from fishing villages within a fishing economy changed utterly by the advent of Tiberias.

Magdala, for example, had been the most important fishing center on the lake before the arrival of Tiberias and, situated as it was just a few miles to the north, its prosperity must have been severely strained by Antipas's new creation. Mary would have known, before she ever heard the voice of Jesus, that the situation was not right, fair, or, more important, the will of God.

Recall what we saw in Chapter 4 about the seismic clash between the tectonic plates of empire and *eschaton* in Daniel 7. In the first century CE those plates carried on their respective surfaces the contemporary kingdom of Rome and—as always—the kingdom of God. But all seismic convulsions—even those that start slowly—take place in very specific place and very particular time. And so it came to pass that it was precisely along the shores of the Sea of Galilee's northwest quadrant—from Tiberias through Magdala and Capernaum to Bethsaida—that the violence of Rome's empire and the nonviolence of God's *eschaton* confronted one another in the 20s of the first common-era century.

We also saw in Chapter 4 that those who opposed Jesus knew that his visionary program had something to do with food, with "eating and drinking," and so they mocked him as a "glutton and a drunkard" (Luke 7:33–34). But his program was actually about who owns the earth, the land, and the lake—God or Rome—and who, therefore, owns the food produced by earth, land, and lake. If "the earth is the Lord's and all that is in it, the world, and those who live in it" (Ps. 24:1), who owns the lake and all the fish in it? If, as God claims, "the land is mine; with me you are but aliens and tenants" (Lev. 25:23), who owns the Sea of *Tiberias*?

Antipas had multiplied the loaves in the valleys around Sepphoris, and he now intended to multiply the fishes in the waters around Tiberias—for the kingdom of Rome. But a magnificently parabolic counterstory tells us how Jesus multiplied the loaves and the fishes—for the kingdom of God.

As I mentioned above, there are six versions of this story in our present New Testament. But for my present purpose I focus on the first one in Mark as the earliest gospel. It begins with this introduction:

They [Jesus and his disciples] went away in the boat to a deserted place [literally, to the desert] by themselves. Now many saw them going and recognized them, and they hurried there on foot from all the towns and arrived ahead of them. As he went ashore, he saw a great crowd; and he had compassion for them, because they were like sheep without a shepherd; and he began to teach them many things. (6:32–34).

Mark takes it for granted that, by God's power, Jesus can do whatever he wants. It is therefore very important to watch carefully what Jesus does and does not do in any given situation. It is necessary, in other words, to read fully and completely the entire story that follows that introduction in 6:32–34. Think of it as a one-act play with five scenes.

Scene 1: Solving the Problem. After a day of teaching, evening approaches, and the problem is where such a large crowd would find food. Two deliberately opposing answers are given to that problem—one from the disciples and the other from Jesus himself:

When it grew late, his disciples came to him and said, "This is a deserted place, and the hour is now very late; *send them away* so that they may go into the surrounding country and villages and buy something for themselves to eat." (6:35–36)

But he answered them, *"You give them something to eat."* They said to him, "Are we to go and buy two hundred denarii worth of bread, and give it to them to eat?" (6:37)

That is a rather fascinating interchange. It sets up the story's intentional confrontation between two solutions: the *disciples'* solution, "send them away," and *Jesus's* solution, "give them something to eat."

That opposition is the core of this narrative and, as the story continues, Jesus brings the disciples repeatedly into the middle between himself and the crowd, so that their solution ("send them away") is changed into his solution ("give them something to eat"). It is, of course, a miracle, but it's a miracle in a parable that emphasizes especially *their* responsibility for the distribution of God's food to God's people. Watch the constant dialectic of "He/Jesus said" and "they/the disciples said" as the story continues.

Scene 2: Seeking the Food. Next, "He said to them, 'How many loaves have you? Go and see.' When they had found out, they said, 'Five, and two fish'" (6:38). In his parallel version, John is somewhat embarrassed at any hint of ignorance from Jesus and rephrases: "Jesus said to Philip, 'Where are we to buy bread for these people to eat?' He said this to test him, for he himself knew what he was going to do" (6:5–6). But John's adaptation also spoils Mark's intention of forcing the disciples repeatedly into the middle between Jesus and the people.

Scene 3: Seating the Crowd. "Then he ordered them to get all the people to sit down in groups on the green grass. So they sat down in groups of hundreds and of fifties" (6:39–40). Once again, the disciples are deliberate intermediaries between Jesus and the crowd. But why that huge time-consuming organization in the midst of a miracle? And why in hundreds and of fifties? Why bother? I hold any answer until later.

Scene 4: Distributing the Food. Even—or especially—at this central moment, the disciples are still intermediaries. "*Taking* the five loaves and the two fish, he looked up to heaven, and *blessed* and *broke* the loaves, and *gave* them to his disciples to set before the people; and he divided the two fish among them all. And all ate and were filled" (6:41–42). Notice those four italicized verbs for future discussion below.

Scene 5: Gathering the Fragments. Afterward "they took up twelve baskets full of broken pieces and of the fish. Those who had eaten the loaves numbered five thousand men" (6:43–44). We can presume that "they" are, once again, the disciples as intermediaries between Jesus and the crowd. Indeed, in this case, John makes that explicit: "When they were satisfied, he told his disciples, 'Gather up the fragments left over, so that nothing may be lost.' So they gathered them up, and from the fragments of the five barley loaves, left by those who had eaten, they filled twelve baskets" (6:12–13).

What exactly is the function of such a detailed narrative? Two elements help us see the purpose. The first element we have seen already. Jesus brings the disciples over to his vision that, with the kingdom of God already present on earth, they are responsible for the adequate distribution of food. "You give them something to eat" prevails over "send them away." And it is indeed striking that the Twelve agree that collaborative eschatology involves teaching the people, but not feeding them. For Jesus, however, the teaching is about feeding.

As already seen so often, the Great Divine Cleanup involves a fair distribution of God's earth for all God's people. But how can anyone else do what Jesus did—if you take the story literally? As told, it is certainly a miracle. But if it is—and I suggest that it is—a miracle in a *parable,* we are asked to think about meaning and implication. This is where a second element becomes equally important.

Jesus could—as Mark certainly believes—have made food suddenly appear, have brought down food from heaven, or even turned stones into bread—for others. Indeed, you might think that a location "in the desert" indicates that Jesus will provide food from heaven as God did in the desert during Israel's Exodus from Egypt (Exod. 16). Furthermore, that awkward division of the people into hundreds and fifties might recall a similar division of the people by Moses during that same Exodus journey (Exod. 18:21, 25). It looked like Mark was preparing us for a new exodus and a new food-from-heaven miracle.

That is not, however, what Jesus did. Instead of any exodus-like option, Jesus multiplied actual food *already there, already present, already available:* "He said to them, 'How many loaves have you? Go and see.' When they had found out, they said, 'Five, and two fish'" (6:38). Why bother with that? Why not just do it from scratch? That is where those four verbs become important:

TAKE → BLESS → BREAK → GIVE

Even when Mark repeats and shortens the story in 8:1–9, he still retains that sequence of those four verbs: "He *took* the seven loaves, and after *giving thanks* he *broke* them and *gave* them to his disciples to distribute; and they distributed them to the crowd" (8:6b–7). Why is their sequence so significant?

I read Mark's *parable* to say that there is more than enough food already present upon our earth when it passes through the hands of divine justice; when it is taken, *blessed,* broken, and given out; when food is seen as God's consecrated gift. The now present kingdom of God is about the equitable distribution of our earth for all. Jesus simply enacts that parable of God as Householder of the World.

I take two elements from that inaugural story in Mark 6:32–44 to pursue throughout the rest of this chapter. A first element is that combination of *bread and fish.* "Bread" is widely used in the biblical tradition as a simple summary for "food," but why keep bringing in "fish"? It is easy to imagine Jesus "breaking" bread, but doing the same to fish is somewhat messier. No wonder, therefore, that in John's version the multiplication story in 6:5–13 is followed by a long discourse on Jesus as the "bread of life" (6:35, 48), but not the "fish of life."

A second element is that fourfold sequence *took, blessed, broke,* and *gave*—in whole or in part. That sequence is too solemn and repetitive not to be significant. It emphasizes that God—through Jesus—has first to *bless* the food or that God—through Jesus—has first to be *given thanks* for the food before Jesus passes it out. It has been thus made sacred or, better, reclaimed for God to whom it had always belonged. I look next at those two elements in that order: first, the *bread and fish,* then the few verbs, *took, blessed* or *gave thanks, broke, gave.*

———

Those six multiplication—better, distribution?—stories about *bread and fish* all take place during the earthly life of Jesus. But there is another story about *bread and fish* from after his earthly life. Well, actually, Luke 5:1–11 has a version of this other story at the very start of Jesus's public life, while John 21:1–14 has it at the very end. Both locations emphasize its importance—either as an inaugural or terminal event in his life here below. But my present focus is on John's postresurrection version.

This revelation of the risen Jesus is the only one ever recorded as taking place at the lake, on the shore of the "Sea of *Tiberias*" (John 21:1). The scene is not set, for example, in a room at Jerusalem, as in Luke 24 and John 20, or on a mountain in Galilee, as in Matthew 28. Instead, in John 21, we are back on the lakeshore to consummate this seismic disturbance where it first began. Here is what happened:

> Gathered there together were Simon Peter, Thomas called the Twin, Nathanael of Cana in Galilee, the sons of Zebedee, and two others of his disciples. Simon Peter said to them, "I am going fishing." They said to him, "We will go with you." They went out and got into the boat, but that night they caught nothing. Just after daybreak, Jesus stood on the beach; but the disciples did not know that it was Jesus. Jesus said to them, "Children, you have no fish, have you?" They answered him, "No." (21:2–5)

Then Jesus tells them where to cast their nets, and they can hardly handle the amount of fish taken at the word of Jesus:

> Jesus said to them, "Cast the net to the right side of the boat, and you will find some." So they cast it, and now they were not able to haul it in because there were so many fish. . . . The other disciples came in the boat, dragging the net full of fish. . . . Simon Peter went aboard and hauled the net ashore, full of large fish, a hundred fifty-three of them; and though there were so many, the net was not torn. (21:6, 8, 11)

There is no consensus on the symbolism of the 153 fish. I myself take it to mean—by whatever symbolism—that Jesus and not Antipas is in control of the lake. It is no longer the Sea of Tiberias; it has become the Sea of Jesus.

In John's story Jesus had already prepared a meal of bread and fish even before their miraculous catch: "When they had gone ashore, they saw a charcoal fire there, with fish on it, and bread" (21:9). Then their fish is added: "Jesus said to them, 'Bring some of the fish that you have just caught'" (21:10).

Of the four verbs, *took, blessed, broke, gave,* in Mark's multiplication story, John has only three somewhat different ones in his version: "Jesus *took* the loaves, and when he had *given thanks,* he *distributed* them to those who were seated; so also the fish, as much as they wanted" (6:11). Those three are reduced to two in the postresurrection catch story: "Jesus came and *took* the bread and *gave* it to them, and did the same with the fish" (21:13). Still, I think, John intends to connect those two meals with Jesus. In other words, what happens before the resurrection continues after it. But what is that?

My proposal is that the kingdom movement of Jesus intends to *take back the lake for God!* It is about the lake as microcosm of the earth, and the question is to whom the lake-as-earth belongs. To Rome or to God? We know that the "bread' of the *Abba* Prayer means *food* in general and not just bread in particular, but with Antipas's establishment of Tiberias to commercialize the lake, to control its fishing industry, and to upgrade his tax bases, food focused on *fish* in the 20s CE.

That is why Jesus was always around nets and boats, fish and fishers, and why there is still so much "fishy stuff" in the gospels. And why that ancient boat is an incarnational symbol of what Tiberias did to Magdala in the first century CE. In the beginning was fish because, when those peasant fishers and fishing villages lost their economy to Antipas's new city of Tiberias, there was first no fish to sell and soon no bread to eat.

One of the temptations refused by Jesus was to turn stones into bread—for himself—after he had fasted forty days in the wilderness. He quoted what Deuteronomy 8:3 says about the manna in the desert: "'One does not live by bread alone, but by every word that comes from the mouth of God'" (Matt. 4:4; Luke 4:4). Of course. But the word from the mouth of God is that all God's people should have a fair share of God's food from God's earth. It is about the just Household of the divine Householder. It is never just about *food*. It is always about *just* food.

———

I have followed that trail of *bread and fish* from Mark 6—as already seen in detail—to John 21, that is, from before to after the resurrection of Jesus. I now do the same for that solemn fourfold verbal sequence *took, blessed* or *gave thanks, broke,* and *gave.* Again the trail starts at Mark 6—already seen—but this time it leads us to Luke 24, that is, once again, from before to after the resurrection.

The walk from Jerusalem to Emmaus and the succeeding meal is found only in Luke's account of Easter Sunday. Two disciples "were going to a village called Emmaus, about seven miles from Jerusalem" (24:13). One of their names is given as Cleopas (24:18) and, following the patriarchal chauvinism of standard Mediterranean custom, the unnamed disciple is most likely his wife.

Jesus joins the couple as they journey along, "but their eyes were kept from recognizing him" (24:16). They tell him of their disappointed hopes concerning "Jesus of Nazareth, who was a prophet mighty in deed and word before God and all the people" (24:19) and, in response, Jesus, "beginning with Moses and all the prophets, interpreted to them the things about himself in all the scriptures" (24:27).

But even that is not enough to allow them to recognize the unknown stranger as Jesus. Looking back later, "they said to each other, 'Were not our hearts burning within us while he was talking to us on the road, while he was opening the scriptures to us?'" (24:32). But even that opening of the scriptures *by* Jesus does not open their eyes *to* Jesus. That only happens with this climax:

As they came near the village to which they were going, he walked ahead as if he were going on. But they urged him strongly, saying, "Stay with us, because it is almost evening and the day is now nearly over." So he went in to stay with them. When he was at the table with them, he *took* bread, *blessed* and *broke* it, and *gave* it to them. Then their eyes were opened, and they recognized him; and he vanished from their sight. (24:28–31)

Why does the couple not evince any surprise at the sudden revelation and equally sudden disappearance of their risen Lord? It is because that story is a fairly obvious *parable* about earliest Christianity's standard ritual in community worship.

First comes the reading of the scriptures. That is necessary, but not enough. It warms the heart, but does not yet reveal the Christ. That happens only when food—and household—is shared with the random stranger. Only then can you announce that Christ "had been made known . . . in the breaking of the bread" (Luke 24:35). Notice, by the way, the word "break." They each could have had individual bread before them at a meal, but that verb emphasizes the *sharing of communal food* rather than the enjoyment of a personal supply.

How are we to understand those three stories—in the desert from Mark, by the lakeshore from John, and at Emmaus from Luke? First of all, that continuity from Jesus before to Jesus after the resurrection is significant. Of all the many things Jesus did before his resurrection, it is that multiplication of *bread and fish* and the invocation of those *four verbs* in Mark that reappears as *bread and fish* in John 21 and as those *four verbs* in Luke 24. Why is that important?

There is, I think, a confrontational edge to that emphasis on "fish." It is not a passing criticism of Antipas from the earthly life of Jesus (Mark 6), but involves what Jesus is and ever remains as the revelation of God. It is, to repeat, about Galilee's lake as a microcosm of God's world—who owns it, controls it, distributes it (John 21). Furthermore, that distribution is by sharing even with—or especially with—the random stranger. Only then is Jesus still present in the Christian community (Luke 24).

I turn next to two other stories that continue and even consummate those preceding three texts. Once again, the first story is set before and the other is set after the resurrection of Jesus. Here the continuity is from Mark in 14:22–25 to Paul in 1 Corinthians 11:20–34.

Mark uses that same fourfold verbal sequence *took, blessed, broke,* and *gave* during what we call the Last Supper and he calls the "Passover meal" (14:14, 16): "While they were eating, he *took* a loaf of bread, and after *blessing* it he *broke* it, *gave* it to them. . . . Then he *took* a cup, and after *giving thanks* he *gave* it to them" (14:22–23). *Passing* the common cup emphasizes, as does *breaking* the common bread, that the symbolism is about sharing communal food and not just consuming individual supplies.

The standard sequence of those four verbs draws our attention to the fact that *bread and fish* has now become *bread and wine.* On the one hand, bread and wine is simply the Mediterranean way of expressing food and drink. Recall, for example, the poetic parallelism in Proverbs about those who "eat the bread of wickedness and drink the wine of violence" (4:17) or are invited to "eat of my bread and drink of the wine I have mixed" (9:5). On the other hand, that sequence of bread and wine allows the equation of bread with the body and wine with the blood of Jesus. Why make that equation?

We think of ordinary death as a separation of body and soul or flesh and spirit. But violent death—for example, execution—is a separation of body and blood. The eucharistic meal recalls that Jesus not only lived for the just distribution of food and drink, but died for insisting on that same thing. He was not demanding charity, generosity, or even hospitality. Rome did not crucify people for those proposals. Jesus was insisting that the world and its food—summarized as bread and wine—belonged to God and not to Rome. For that he died violently on a cross—so that "bread and wine" led to "body and blood."

It follows, therefore, that Christians participating in the Lord's Supper are *collaborating* with the justice of God as revealed in the life and death of Christ. Jesus says nothing about his substitution for us, but rather invites our participation with him. "He took a cup," for example, "and after giving thanks he gave it to them, and all of them drank from it" (Mark 14:23). So how exactly does that work out in practice? One answer comes from Paul, writing on that very question to the Corinthians.

Roman householders often gave feasts that included not only their social equals, but also their freed slaves, clients, and assorted hangers-on. That was, of course, a deliberate display of hierarchical power. But at such banquets, Roman moralists asked, should all get the same food and drink? Some said of course not. At the end of the first century CE, the poet Martial—who would eventually flee Rome for his native Spain—complained bitterly in his *Epigrams* about such calculated social humiliation. "Let us eat," he demanded, "the same fare" (3.60).

Others said yes, of course. One of Martial's patrons was the very aristocratic Pliny the Younger. He insisted indignantly in his *Letters* that his custom was "to give all my company the same fare." But that meant, he continued, "that my freed slaves do not drink the same wine I do—but *I* drink what *they* do" (2.6). "Social equality" there was cultural slumming. And that was the problem Paul ran into with the eucharistic meal at Corinth.

The original title "Lord's Supper" meant the Lord's style of supper, that is, a share-meal where all alike got enough of the same food and drink. Equality in Christ meant equality in menu. It was not, of course, our symbolic morsel and sip, but a true meal. What happened at Corinth was that the drag of cultural normalcy pulled the Lord's Supper back into Roman hierarchical expectations.

When the various small Christian communities of Corinth celebrated the Lord's Supper together at the home of a better-off member, the nonworking "haves" arrived early and ate the upper-class food and drink that they brought. When the "have-nots" arrived later after the day's work, they had to make do with what was left. Paul is, to put it mildly, not pleased with them:

When you come together, it is not really to eat the Lord's supper. For when the time comes to eat, each of you goes ahead with your own supper, and one goes hungry and another becomes drunk. What! Do you not have homes to eat and drink in? Or do you show contempt for the church of God and humiliate those who have nothing? (1 Cor. 11:20–22)

What is his solution? He begins by insisting that his own understanding of the Lord's Supper is very traditional:

I received from the Lord what I also handed on to you, that the Lord Jesus on the night when he was betrayed *took* a loaf of bread, and when he had *given thanks,* he *broke* it and said, "This is my body that is for you. Do this in remembrance of me." In the same way he took the cup also, *after supper,* saying, "This cup is the new covenant in my blood. Do this, as often as you drink it, in remembrance of me." (1 Cor. 11:23–25)

Once again, we have three of those four verbs, *took, gave thanks,* and *broke; gave* is left implicit. But what I especially emphasize is that phrase "after supper."

That sequence of first the bread-as-body, then the supper, and finally the wine-as-blood puts the supper in the middle. The haves cannot come and have their better supper first and then celebrate the eucharistic meal with whatever bread and wine is left over. The full and very real supper is in the center of the symbolic ritual.

From bread and fish to bread and wine, from the life to the death of Jesus, from before to after the resurrection, it is always about God's food in God's world for God's people. All of that is packed into the simple challenge of "Give us this day our daily bread." The Lord's Supper is already present in the Lord's Prayer.

When *we* read or hear, "Give us this day our daily bread," that simple word "bread" carries with it all those share-meals with Jesus during his life, before his death, and after his resurrection. It contains the multiplication meal, the Emmaus meal, the lakeside meal, and the eucharistic meal. It is the daily bread of daily justice along with the daily danger of challenging daily injustice.

But, despite the almost cliché status of "our daily bread" in English (just try an Advanced Search for the phrase on Google), the Greek is strikingly unusual. It is literally:

> The bread of us the daily (*epiousian*) give to us today. (Matt. 6:11)

All the other units in the *Abba* Prayer start with the verb involved: "be hallowed," "be come," "be done," "forgive," "do not bring." But here the "bread" comes first, and then the adjective "daily" (*epiousian*) gets special emphasis, as in that preceding literal articulation.

The adjective *epiousia* is found in the New Testament only in Matthew 6:11 and Luke 11:3. Our major Greek dictionary translates it: "the coming day, sufficient for the day . . . from *hē epiousia hēmera,* the coming day." The meaning is: enough for today, but also with assurance of the same for tomorrow. It is a request that "our daily bread" be never again exceptional or conditional as in the past, but always normal and unconditional in the present and the future.

The best way to understand that vision of "our daily bread" is to go back before the *Abba* Prayer or any of those meals with Jesus—during his life, before his death, or after his resurrection—to the far older story of the "bread from heaven," in the desert during the Exodus of the Israelites from Egypt. It is daily bread as bread daily.

You will recall, from Chapter 3, that the Priestly tradition moved from Sabbath creation through Sabbath day and Sabbath year to climax with Sabbath jubilee. That same tradition created a magnificent parable to sum it all up and located it during the Exodus from Egypt. It is a vision of the Sabbath day, but also of how God distributes food as manna/bread for all. It is also the best commentary on "our *daily* bread" in the *Abba* Prayer of Jesus as meaning *enough bread for today, and tomorrow, and every day to come.*

The people complained of hunger in the desert, and "the Lord said to Moses, 'I am going to rain bread from heaven for you'" (Exod. 16:4). The promise is that "you shall have your fill of bread; then you shall know that I am the Lord your God" (16:12). When the manna appeared, the people "said to one another, 'What is it?' [Hebrew *man hu'*, hence *manna*]. For they did not know what it was. Moses said to them, 'It is the bread that the Lord has given you to eat'" (16:15).

The manna is quite simply God's bread, but there are five very precise instructions for harvesting this miraculous food from heaven:

The Lord said to Moses, "I am going to rain bread from heaven for you, and each day the people shall go out and gather enough for that day." (16:4)

"On the sixth day, when they prepare what they bring in, it will be twice as much as they gather on other days.". . . On the sixth day they gathered twice as much food. (16:5, 22)

"Gather as much of it as each of you needs, an omer [about a half gallon] to a person according to the number of persons, all providing for those in their own tents." The Israelites did so, some gathering more, some less. But when they measured it with an omer, those who gathered much had nothing over, and those who gathered little had no shortage; they gathered as much as each of them needed. . . . Morning by morning they gathered it, as much as each needed. (16:16–18, 21)

"Let no one leave any of it over until morning." But . . . some left part of it until morning, and it bred worms and became foul. (16:19–20)

On the seventh day some of the people went out to gather, and they found none. (16:27)

Those parabolic emphases are quite clear. When God directly distributes food there is enough for each and every day (*daily* bread?); there is miraculously the same amount for each person per day no matter what each takes; there is no hoarding because it spoils overnight; there is no food even present on the Sabbath, but twice as much the day before; but when that pre-Sabbath bread is kept overnight, it "[does] not become foul, and there [are] no worms in it" (16:24).

There is, however, one very interesting aspect to the people's "fill of bread" (16:8, 12), to "the bread that the Lord has given them to eat" (16:15). It is the householder who is commanded by God to pick up enough bread for the entire household each morning: "Gather as much of it as each of you needs . . . according to the number of persons, all providing for those in their own tents" (16:16). It is, as always, about the householder and the house as microcosm of the Householder and the House.

We are now ready to move to the prayer's next challenge, and this book's next chapter. What will it be? What, in fact, must it be? Every peasant farmer or city artisan as well as every decent landlord or good emperor would have known immediately the answer to that question. The other side of enough food for today is no debt for tomorrow.

Here is an example on the imperial level. Rome's ancient Senate House, the Curia Julia, now contains two large bas-reliefs from the time of the emperor Trajan at the start of the second century CE. They were originally located outside in the Forum, but are now better protected by the Curia's covered roof.

One of the images is of Trajan distributing *food* to the orphaned children of Rome. Those are symbolized by a woman with a baby in her arms coming toward his seated figure. The other image shows a line of people carrying *debt* tablets to the emperor to be burned at his feet. With those records gone, the debts are expunged.

Enough food for today must also involve no debt for tomorrow. So, a hundred years before Trajan, Jesus connects food—positively—and debt—negatively—in his *Abba* Prayer. But notice one other feature of that transition from bread to debt and on to temptation.

The prayer's first half on God's name, kingdom, and will had no "ands" between them. Each of those three challenges involved the other ones even despite a deliberate climax in presentation. God's name cannot be hallowed except through the coming of God's kingdom, which results in God's eternal will being done on earth. But the prayer's second half is cumulative; hence those "ands" between bread and debt as well as between debt and temptation. It is not about bread *or* debt *or* temptation, but about all three together in a crescendo. So what comes next after "Give us our daily bread" is—and must be— "*and* forgive us our debts."

7

Forgive Us Our Debts

And forgive us our debts, as we forgive our debtors.

Matthew 6:12, KJV

And forgive us our debts, as we also have forgiven our debtors.

Matthew 6:12, NRSV

"The French have only come," Napoleon Bonaparte told the Egyptians at Alexandria on July 12, 1798, "to rescue the rights of the poor from the grasp of their tyrants," since "all men are equal in the eyes of God." Precisely a year into that "rescue" of Egyptian peasants from Ottoman Turks by French dragoons, a soldier, digging fortifications at Rosetta, about forty miles east of Alexandria, found a 4-by-3-foot inscription written in Egyptian—in both sacred hieroglyphics and popular cursive script—and in classical Greek.

After the British defeated the French, that "Rosetta Stone" ended up in London's British Museum rather than in Paris's Louvre. It has never—so far—been exhibited in Cairo's Egyptian Museum, where a copy serves as reminder of its true origin. It was, however, in France that Jean-François Champollion, having taught himself Hebrew, Latin, and Greek, used the Greek section of the Rosetta Stone to crack the other two Egyptian scripts.

The inscription dates from 196 BCE during the strife-torn reign of the boy-king Ptolemy IV Epiphanes, under whom Judea passed from

Egyptian control—forever—to Syrian control—but not forever. Here is the section of present interest:

> **WHEREAS** King Ptolemy, the Ever-Living, the Beloved of Ptah, the God Epiphanes Eucharistos . . . being a god sprung from a god and goddess like Horus the son of Isis and Osiris . . . has wholly remitted some of the revenues and taxes levied in Egypt and has lightened others in order that the people and all the others might be in prosperity during his reign; and
>
> **whereas** he has remitted the debts to the crown being many in number which they in Egypt and the rest of the kingdom owed . . .

In that text the first two points mentioned are the mitigation of taxes and the remission of debts as the new ruler "apportioned justice to all."

Go back now from 196 BCE to 1760 BCE and from the Egyptian hieroglyphics of the Rosetta Stone to the Babylonian laws of the Code of Hammurabi. The latter, engraved on a slab of black diorite 7 feet tall, was taken at the start of the twelfth century BCE from the Amorite capital at Babylon to the Elamite capital at Susa—as the spoils of invasion. Thence it was taken at the start of the twentieth century to Paris's Louvre Museum—as the spoils of excavation. There is now, as with the Rosetta Stone in the Cairo museum, only a copy of the Code of Hammurabi in Iraq's National Museum at Baghdad.

Hammurabi ruled the Old Babylonian Empire from 1728 to 1686 BCE, and his law code is the fullest one still extant from the ancient Mesopotamian world. At the top is a bas-relief of Hammurabi himself as he receives the legal prescriptions from the god of justice, the sun god Shamash. The prologue asserts that Hammurabi has been divinely appointed "to bring about the rule of righteousness in the land, to destroy the wicked and the evildoers; so that the strong should not harm the weak." The epilogue repeats that divine mandate: "that the strong might not injure the weak, in order to protect the widows and orphans . . . in order to declare justice in the land, to settle all disputes, and heal all injuries."

In between those framing declarations are 282 case laws ("If . . ."), and this is the one of present interest:

> If any one fail to meet a claim for debt, and sell himself, his wife, his son, and daughter for money or give them away to forced labor: they shall work for three years in the house of the man who bought them, or the proprietor, and in the fourth year they shall be set free. (#117)

That law is not just about release from taxes or debts, as on the Rosetta Stone, but about release from debt slavery itself. No matter how great the unpaid debt, the resulting slavery and forced labor could only last for three full years. It is, as it were, an early version of our limited liability law.

The legal codes of the biblical Torah continued that ancient Mesopotamian tradition. They involve justice descending from heaven to earth; the king as its divine incarnation; release from tax and debt, interest and slavery; and special concern for the most vulnerable ones—the poor and the oppressed, the widows, orphans, and resident aliens.

There is, however, one magnificently unique feature of that divine vision of distributive justice and restorative righteousness in its biblical realization. There, as seen in Chapter 3, the metronome of time itself—its days, years, and centuries—beats to the rhythm of the divine justice from Sabbath creation through Sabbath day and Sabbath year to Sabbath jubilee.

My primary focus in this chapter is on debt and its forgiveness. But in the biblical tradition debt, slavery, and slavery for debt are very closely connected. In debt slavery persons are sold into temporary or permanent slavery to pay off debt. That type of forced-labor enslavement was described almost four millennia ago in the Code of

Hammurabi—as we read above—and taken up into the covenantal theology of Israel from that Mesopotamian tradition.

That interaction of debt and slavery and especially of slavery for debt in the biblical tradition raises a secondary focus for this chapter. Debt slavery makes me wonder if in our contemporary world those places where slavery is forbidden by law have simply replaced it with excessive debt as neoslavery. Maybe excessive debt is a far better way of owning or controlling individuals and nations than old-fashioned forms of direct slavery and direct colonialism?

Within that biblical tradition—and everywhere else as well?—*debt* leads easily into *slavery*. But with or as debt comes *interest* or *pledge*. I begin therefore with interest or pledge as possibly leading to excessive debt in the Bible:

INTEREST or PLEDGE → DEBT → SLAVERY

Interest is a fee charged for borrowing money, usually a percent of the total. A pledge is something, chattel or real estate, surrendered as security against money borrowed. Defaulting on a loan leads to loss of collateral—for example, the family farm—or to debt enslavement for some or all of its members. I look first at interest and pledge in the Old Testament, then at debt slavery.

As a possible way to halt the trajectory moving from interest through debt to slavery, the Torah forbids interest on help or subsistence loans to neighbors (including "resident aliens"), but not on trade or commerce loans to foreigners:

> If any of your kin fall into difficulty and become dependent on you, you shall support them; they shall live with you as though resident aliens. Do not take interest in advance or otherwise make a profit from them, but fear your God; let them live with you. You shall not lend them your money at interest taken in advance, or provide them food at a profit. I am the Lord your God, who brought you out of the land of Egypt, to give you the land of Canaan, to be your God. (Lev. 25:35–38)

On loans to a foreigner you may charge interest, but on loans to another Israelite you may not charge interest, so that the Lord your God may bless you in all your undertakings in the land that you are about to enter and possess. (Deut. 23:20)

As always, the model for such things as noninterest loans is God's deliverance of the Israelites from those Egyptian "taskmasters set over them to oppress them with forced labor" (Exod. 1:11) followed by the gift of the land of Canaan as their inheritance.

The legal theory is clear. If a fellow Israelite is desperate enough to need help, it should be offered freely. There should be no interest on money loaned and no profit made for food given. So much for theory, but what about actual practice? Was that all dreamy idealism or did it involve practical observances? We get a good glimpse of that in a later historical situation.

At the start of the sixth century BCE, the Babylonian Empire conquered Israel, destroyed Solomon's Temple, and took Jerusalem's aristocratic leadership into what became known as the Babylonian exile. By the middle of that same century, however, the Persians had defeated the Babylonians. Israel's exiled leaders were sent home to put the country back on its feet as a tax-paying dependency of the new Persian Empire.

At first all was wild enthusiasm. One prophet even called Cyrus the Great, emperor of Persia, the awaited messiah of God (Isa. 45:1). The general imperial policy involved the restoration of the devastated homeland, the reconsecration of the ruined Temple, and the reinstitution of ancestral laws. Babylonian attack-and-loot was to be replaced by Persian revive-and-tax. Israel was especially important as a buffer on the border with Egypt.

In 445 BCE, one hundred years after the restoration began, Persia sent a Jewish governor named Nehemiah to speed up the process of reestablishing the country. Since the Torah was Israel's ancestral law, what did he do about reclaiming the Torah? What happened to the Torah's ideals about interest, pledge, and debt in that Persian-decreed restoration of ancestral law? How were things, for example, between the newly returned families of the "haves" and the families of the "have-nots" who never left? Here is what happened as "have-nots" protested against the "haves":

> There was a great outcry of the people and of their wives [the "have-nots"] against their Jewish kin [the "haves"]. For there were those who said, "With our sons and our daughters, we are many; we must get grain, so that we may eat and stay alive." There were also those who said, "We are having to pledge our fields, our vineyards, and our houses in order to get grain during the famine." And there were those who said, "We are having to borrow money on our fields and vineyards to pay the king's tax. Now our flesh is the same as that of our kindred; our children are the same as their children; and yet we are forcing our sons and daughters to be slaves, and some of our daughters have been ravished; we are powerless, and our fields and vineyards now belong to others." (Neh. 5:1–5)

"After thinking it over," Nehemiah said, "I brought charges against the nobles and the officials; I said to them, 'You are all taking interest from your own people.' And I called a great assembly to deal with them" (5:7). This is his decree:

> I and my brothers and my servants are lending them money and grain. Let us stop this taking of interest. Restore to them, this very day, their fields, their vineyards, their olive orchards, and their houses, and the interest on money, grain, wine, and oil that you have been exacting from them. (5:10–11)

The aristocracy of nobles, officials, and priests accepted his decree and swore to follow it not only with distributive justice for the future, but also with restorative justice for the past. A half millennium later, the deuterocanonical 4 Maccabees summed it up succinctly: "As soon as one adopts a way of life in accordance with the law, even though a lover of money, one is forced to act contrary to natural ways and to lend without interest to the needy and to cancel the debt when the seventh year arrives" (2:8).

Notice, however, that distinction between *interest* and *pledge* in those texts from Nehemiah and also that *both* are revoked. Some of the aristocracy demanded interest on loans to the peasantry despite those laws seen above from Leviticus 25 and Deuteronomy 22. Others respected those laws, but demanded a pledge instead (usually the family farm), which would be taken if the loan was defaulted on. Pledges against default could be far more damaging than interest on loans. That is why the biblical tradition, although it doesn't forbid pledges, seeks at least to control the social havoc of pledges—large or small. For example:

No one shall take a mill or an upper millstone in pledge, for that would be taking a life in pledge. . . . When you make your neighbor a loan of any kind, you shall not go into the house to take the pledge. You shall wait outside, while the person to whom you are making the loan brings the pledge out to you. If the person is poor, you shall not sleep in the garment given you as the pledge. You shall give the pledge back by sunset, so that your neighbor may sleep in the cloak and bless you. . . . You shall not take a widow's garment in pledge. (Deut. 24:6, 10–13, 17)

Unfortunately, therefore, even the eradication of interest on help loans cannot stop the accumulation of debt. It is simple enough to avoid *interest* on a loan—especially on a short-term one—and replace it with a *penalty* for default. Your land or labor is still collateral and can still be acquired upon failure to repay on time. And the amount of such default penalties may be far harsher than any interest payments. It is still necessary, therefore, for the Torah to face the second element in that unholy sequence from interest or pledge to debt and from debt to debt slavery.

———

You will recall the sequence in Chapter 3 from Sabbath creation through Sabbath day and Sabbath year to Sabbath jubilee. The days, years, and centuries of human time were thereby absorbed—as just mentioned—into the divine rhythm of distributive justice and restorative righteousness. I mentioned there that the Sabbath year had three aspects—resting fields, remitting debts, and freeing debt slaves—and that the last two would be discussed in this chapter.

I return then, as promised, to the Sabbath year within God's dream of God's world for all God's people. I begin with debt slavery within the oldest legal section of the Bible, that is, the Book of the Covenant in Exodus 20:22–23:33. It opens, as you might imagine, like this: "I am the Lord your God, who brought you out of the land of Egypt, out of the house of slavery" (20:2). So, having been liberated from slavery as a people, how can one Israelite ever—permanently—enslave another Israelite? Hence, this decree about male slaves:

> When you buy a male Hebrew slave, he shall serve six years, but in the seventh he shall go out a free person, without debt. If he comes in single, he shall go out single; if he comes in married, then his wife shall go out with him. If his master gives him a wife and she bears him sons or daughters, the wife and her children shall be her master's and he shall go out alone. But if the slave declares, "I love my master, my wife, and my children; I will not go out a free person," then his master shall bring him before God. He shall be brought to the door or the doorpost; and his master shall pierce his ear with an awl; and he shall serve him for life. (Exod. 21:2–6)

You will notice that Hammurabi's law on debt slavery is twice as generous as that in the Bible. His maximum enslavement for debt is three years, but the Bible's is six years. The reason is probably not that the Bible intends to be twice as severe as Hammurabi. It is probably that it wants to connect the freedom of debt slaves with the Sabbath year, which comes every seventh year. There could never be *more* than six years of enslavement before a Sabbath year ended it.

The law for female debt slaves is different because of the obvious possibility of sexual exploitation. Males may have been out the time and labor they spent in servitude, but female slaves may have been raped or rendered unlikely to find a marriage partner after their release:

> When a man sells his daughter as a slave, she shall not go out as the male slaves do. If she does not please her master, who designated her for himself, then he shall let her be redeemed; he shall have no right to sell her to a foreign people, since he has dealt unfairly with her. If he designates her for his son, he shall deal with her as with a daughter. If he takes another wife to himself, he shall not diminish the food, clothing, or marital rights of the first wife. And if he does not do these three things for her, she shall go out without debt, without payment of money. (Exod. 21:7–11)

The reason behind that release of debt slaves is, of course, the very character of God as experienced by Israel in its release from forced labor in Egypt.

Thus, a century and a half before the governor Nehemiah, according to the prophet Jeremiah, God said, "I myself made a covenant with your ancestors when I brought them out of the land of Egypt, out of the house of slavery, saying, 'Every seventh year each of you must set free any Hebrews who have been sold to you and have served you six years; you must set them free from your service'" (34:13–14).

A second proclamation of those laws about release from debt slavery is
found in Deuteronomy. This is the last of the five books of the Torah,
and in it the added specifications and expansions are very interesting.
Notice especially that a seventh-year release of *debts themselves* is commanded (15:1–11) even before any mention of a seventh-year freedom
for *debt slaves* (15:12–18). With regard to debts:

> Every seventh year you shall grant a remission of debts. And
> this is the manner of the remission: every creditor shall remit
> the claim that is held against a neighbor, not exacting it of a
> neighbor who is a member of the community, because the Lord's
> remission has been proclaimed. Of a foreigner you may exact it,
> but you must remit your claim on whatever any member of your
> community owes you. (Deut. 15:1–3)

That is the distinction seen above between help loans for neighbors and trade loans for foreigners. The "resident alien" is, of course,
a "neighbor" and not a "foreigner." There is also an added warning
against refusing to make any loans when "the year of remission is
near" (15:9–10). But what comes next is the most striking difference
between debt-slavery release in Exodus 21 and that in Deuteronomy 15.
With regard to debt slaves:

> If a member of your community, whether a Hebrew man or a
> Hebrew woman, is sold to you and works for you six years, in
> the seventh year you shall set that person free. And when you
> send a male slave out from you a free person, you shall not send
> him out empty-handed. Provide liberally out of your flock, your
> threshing floor, and your wine press, thus giving to him some of
> the bounty with which the Lord your God has blessed you. *Re-*
> *member that you were a slave in the land of Egypt, and the Lord your*
> *God redeemed you; for this reason I lay this command upon you today.*
> Do not consider it a hardship when you send them out from you

free persons, because for six years they have given you services worth [twice] the wages of hired laborers; and the Lord your God will bless you in all that you do. (Deut. 15:12–15, 18)

That is a fascinating expansion over the release from debt slavery just seen in the older laws of Exodus 21. But it is also a logical extension of that Exodus model as the archetypal release of Israel from Egyptian slave labor.

Notice that italicized sentence (15:15). It recalls the inaugural Exodus experience of release, freedom, and liberation as model for debt-slavery release. Also, that opening phrase, "you shall set that person free" (15:12), is more literally "you shall let that person go." That, of course, recalls the more famous repeated command of God through Moses to Pharaoh: "Let my people go" (Exod. 5:1–10:4).

Furthermore, the command that "you shall not send *him* out empty-handed" (15:13), rephrased as "send *them* out from you free persons" (15:18), picks up the term "empty-handed" from the time of the Exodus:

I will bring this people into such favor with the Egyptians that, when you go, you will not go *empty-handed;* each woman shall ask her neighbor and any woman living in the neighbor's house for jewelry of silver and of gold, and clothing, and you shall put them on your sons and on your daughters; and so you shall plunder the Egyptians. (Exod. 3:21–22; see 12:35–36)

That "plunder" is simply the back pay and "damages" due to those who have been enslaved. Some nations do it willingly, some unwillingly, and some never.

Finally, Deuteronomy 15 vacillates between two ideal visions on this whole subject of debts. Compare this magnificent contradiction:

There will, however, be no one in need among you, because the Lord is sure to bless you in the land that the Lord your God is giving you as a possession to occupy. (15:4)

Since there will never cease to be some in need on the earth,
I therefore command you, "Open your hand to the poor and
needy neighbor in your land." (15:11)

Both parts of that last sentence are implicitly cited by Jesus in
Mark 14:7: "You always have the poor with you, and you can show
kindness to them whenever you wish." However, with both Deuteronomy 15:11 and Mark 14:7, the whole verse must always be cited. It
is very unfortunate that we often hear only the abbreviated version,
"You always have the poor with you" from Matthew 26:11 and John
12:8. The absolutely nonbiblical result is often complacency with
what is then interpreted as a divinely constituted inequality that demands not justice for all, but—at best—charity for some.

———

Everything seen so far about the *Abba* Prayer of Jesus has shown it
to be a hymnic summary of the distributive justice and restorative
righteousness of the biblical God. That theme reverberates from one
end of the Christian Old Testament to the other. Indeed, it is always
the very *character* of the divine Householder that is at stake. That
character was revealed in God's archetypal release of Israel from slavery in Egypt. That external release is the permanent model for the
internal release from slavery of fellow Israelites. The biblical God did
not oppose Egypt because it was not Israel, but because it was not
just. Equal opposition would have awaited Israel from God if it had
become the new Egypt.

From all of those preceding examples, I have one general conclusion. Prayed within that biblical matrix, "Forgive us our debts, as
we also have forgiven our debtors" should be taken literally and not
metaphorically. Those examples spelled out in very precise detail
how literal debts were to be forgiven, erased among human beings.
But for God to forgive us our *literal* debts, we must owe God *literal*
debts, so what are those *literal* debts? What—literally—do we owe
to God?

In that Sabbath-crowned creation, as seen already in Chapter 3, people are created *in God's image* as stewards of the world:

> Let us make humankind in our image, according to our like-
> ness; and let them have dominion over the fish of the sea, and
> over the birds of the air, and over the cattle, and over all the
> wild animals of the earth, and over every creeping thing that
> creeps upon the earth. (Gen. 1:26)

We humans are *image* stewards of God. We are created, in other words, to run God's world with God, through God, and in God. Just so, in microcosm, and again as already seen, God tells Israel: "The land is mine; with me you are but aliens and tenants" (Lev. 25:23). Furthermore, and again as already seen, Paul rephrased our dignity as "images of God" by calling us "heirs of God." As divine heirs, we are responsible, Paul concluded, never to increase but always to alleviate the "groaning of creation" (Rom. 8:17–22).

Images and heirs, stewards and managers, tenant farmers and resi-dent aliens owe literal debts to the owners of their assigned properties. And that debt is to do and produce whatever the owner expects of them.

We owe it to God to run God's world responsibly. We owe the divine Householder the conservation of the world house; we owe the divine Homemaker the consecration of the earth home. We owe God adequate care of all God's creation. We owe God collaboration in hallowing God's name, in establishing God's kingdom, and in doing God's will "as in heaven so also on earth." We owe it to God to cease focusing on heaven, especially in order to avoid focusing on earth. We owe it to God to ensure that there is enough food and not too much debt in God's well-run Household.

I concluded the last chapter with the parable of the daily bread, from Exodus 16. I now conclude this section of this one with the parable of the debt release, from Jeremiah 34. By *parable* I mean a story that is not given as history, but is asserted as challenge.

The parable is set immediately before the Babylonian exile. It concerns Zedekiah, the last king of Judah, who rebelled against the Neo-Babylonian Empire in 586 BCE. The Babylonian king Nebuchadnezzar "slaughtered the sons of Zedekiah before his eyes, then put out the eyes of Zedekiah; they bound him in fetters and took him to Babylon" (2 Kings 25:7) along with all of Judah's aristocratic leadership. Think of the story as another one-act play, but this time with three scenes. Here is *Scene 1:*

> King Zedekiah had made a covenant with all the people in Jerusalem to make a proclamation of liberty to them, that all should set free their Hebrew slaves, male and female, so that no one should hold another Judean in slavery. And they obeyed, all the officials and all the people who had entered into the covenant that all would set free their slaves, male or female, so that they would not be enslaved again; they obeyed and set them free. But afterward they turned around and took back the male and female slaves they had set free, and brought them again into subjection as slaves. (Jer. 34:8–11)

That's a rather heavy-handed scene, and at this point in this chapter you can probably write the next ones for yourself.

In *Scene 2,* God, as expected, emphasizes that the divine model for this covenant of release from debt slavery is the release from Egyptian bondage:

> Thus says the Lord, the God of Israel: I myself made a covenant with your ancestors when I brought them out of the land of Egypt, out of the house of slavery, saying, "Every seventh year each of you must set free any Hebrews who have been sold to you and have served you six years; you must set them free from

your service." But your ancestors did not listen to me or incline
their ears to me. (34:13–14)

Clearly, of course, the people have acknowledged their duty, accepted
it, and then, to make matters much, much worse, retracted and defaulted on it. It is, as I say, heavy-handed, but thereby also quite clear.
After that, God warns that their action of taking back the slaves
has "profaned" God's name (34:16)—remember God's name from
Chapter 3?

And then comes *Scene 3:*

Therefore, thus says the Lord: You have not obeyed me by
granting a release to your neighbors and friends; I am going to
grant a release to you, says the Lord—a release to the sword, to
pestilence, and to famine. I will make you a horror to all the
kingdoms of the earth. . . . [Your] corpses shall become food for
the birds of the air and the wild animals of the earth. . . . The
towns of Judah I will make a desolation without inhabitant.
(34:17–22)

In that parable the very reason for the Babylonian exile was an alleged
acceptance and then a rejection of the Sabbath year "release" from
debt and debt slavery.

In that parable the Sabbath year's release from debt slavery is judged
so important that defaulting on it is the specific reason for Babylon's
imperial devastation of Israel. Recall that incident on debt release seen
above in Nehemiah 5? The Zedekiah and Nehemiah stories frame the
Babylonian exile by citing the nonremission of debt as its cause beforehand and the remission of debt as its remedy afterward.

———

That *literal* understanding of debt as what one owes to God or neighbor seems immediately obvious as Israel's biblical tradition flows into

and through the *Abba* Prayer of Jesus. It also represents that *literal* hope for enough bread today and no debt tomorrow that has been the ancient dream of the earth's "have-nots."

But I think it fair to say that many (most?) Christians saying the Lord's Prayer take those "debts" metaphorically rather than literally. "Debts" mean "sins," and we are asking God to "forgive us our sins as we forgive those who sin against us." Maybe all that preceding talk of literal debt and literal remission of debt and debt slavery is mistaken? How can we tell what was intended by Jesus and what was intended by the gospel writers?

First, I begin with Mark. We already said that he may have known a version of this prayer. You will remember, from Chapter 5, how Jesus invoked God as *Abba* in submitting to God's "will" in Gethsemane (14:36). Mark also says: "Whenever you stand praying, forgive, if you have anything against anyone; so that your Father in heaven may also forgive you your trespasses" (11:25). That, by the way, is the only time Mark ever uses the standard Matthean phrase "your Father in heaven" (literally, "in the heavens"). I think with the word "trespasses" Mark is already moving from "debts" in the direction of "sins."

Second, I continue with Matthew. In his version of the Lord's Prayer, he uses "debts" twice (6:12). But immediately after concluding the prayer, he adds this: "For if you forgive others their trespasses, your heavenly Father will also forgive you; but if you do not forgive others, neither will your Father forgive your trespasses" (6:14–15). "Debts" have become "trespasses."

Furthermore, Matthew takes up this question of divine and human forgiveness once again in 18:15, 21–35. He opens by speaking about the procedure to follow: "If another member of the church *sins* against you" (18:15). Then Peter asks Jesus a question: "Lord, if another member of the church *sins* against me, how often should I forgive? As many as seven times?" Jesus replies, "Not seven times, but, I tell you, seventy-seven times" (18:21–22). It is quite clear that we are not talking about "debts" or "trespasses" here, but about "sins."

Next, Matthew gives us a parable about *literal* debts. It begins, "A king . . . wished to settle accounts with his slaves" (18:23). The first debtor owed him the huge amount of "ten thousand talents" and, since he was unable to pay, the king "ordered him to be sold, together with his wife and children and all his possessions, and payment to be made" (18:24–25; a good example, by the way, of enslavement for debt). But when the debtor begged for mercy, the debt was totally remitted. This debtor then went to another who owed him a mere "hundred denarii" and, despite his own experience with the king's forgiveness, he disregarded the second debtor's pleas for mercy and "threw him into prison until he would pay the debt" (18:30). Infuriated by the first debtor's actions, the king "handed him over to be tortured until he would pay his entire debt" (18:34).

Finally, Matthew ends the parable with this: "So my heavenly Father will also do to every one of you, if you do not forgive your brother or sister from your heart" (18:35). In this case, literal *debt* is a parabolic metaphor for *sin*. In terms of divine and human forgiveness, Matthew moves from "debts" (6:12) to "trespasses" (6:24–15) to "sins" (18:15, 21–35).

I conclude with Luke. His version of the Lord's Prayer leaves out two sections present in Matthew and *The Teaching* (see the Appendix): "Your will be done, on earth as it is in heaven" and "rescue us from the evil one." But he also makes one very significant change in what he retains:

> And forgive us our sins,
>   for we ourselves forgive everyone indebted to us. (Luke 11:4)

Matthew works from "debts" through "trespasses" to "sins," but Luke gets there right away. But, of course, he still retains "indebted to us" rather than "sinning against us."

I have three conclusions from all of that textual activity. One is that "debts" was originally intended quite literally. Jesus meant that eternal peasant dyad of enough bread for today and no debt for tomorrow. Were it originally and clearly metaphorical—"debts" meaning "sins"—everyone would have understood that intention and the progression in terminology from "debts" to "trespasses" to "sins" would not have been necessary.

Another is that, from Mark through Matthew and into Luke, "debts" change to "trespasses" and then to "sins." In its present format, therefore, it seems advisable to read Matthew's text as including *both* debt *and* sin—not debt alone, not sin alone, and certainly not sin instead of debt, but both together. Indeed, the ultimate challenge may be to ponder their interaction. And, at least for the biblical tradition, when debt creates too much inequality, it has become sinful.

Finally, I want to think one last time about "And forgive us our debts/sins, as we also *have* forgiven our debtors/sinners" in Matthew's version of the *Abba* Prayer. For Matthew that seems to be not just a *comparison*—as God forgives, so must we forgive—but a *condition*—God will forgive, only if we forgive.

That conditional aspect of forgiveness is made very explicit by the negative interpretation added at the end of the Lord's Prayer in Matthew:

> For if you forgive others their trespasses, your heavenly Father will also forgive you;
> but if you do not forgive others, neither will your Father forgive your trespasses. (6:14–15)

In the Lord's Prayer the sequence is divine forgiveness and then human forgiveness, as a simple comparison. But in that addition the sequence is reversed and made into an emphatic condition. If we do not forgive others, neither will God forgive us.

Finally, Matthew 18 uses the parable of two debtors to make that same point. I repeat its ending:

In anger his lord handed him over to be tortured until he would pay his entire debt. So my heavenly Father will also do to every one of you, if you do not forgive your brother or sister from your heart. (18:34–35)

Is it true that God will forgive us everything except our own unforgiveness? But of all the things for which we need divine forgiveness, we need it above all else for our lack of human forgiveness.

I conclude that, whether you read Matthew 6:12 in the Lord's Prayer as about debts or sins, divine forgiveness is never conditional and should not be interpreted with either 6:14–15 or 18:15, 21–35. The question is not whether God will forgive this or that sin, but whether there is anything that God will not forgive, even—or especially—our lack of human forgiveness.

————

I turn now in transition to the prayer's final challenge—temptation. At the end of Chapter 5, on bread, it was relatively easy to guess the subject of the next chapter, debt. The positive ideal of enough bread for today and the negative one of no debt for tomorrow are standard hopes of the "have-nots" of history. But what should the third challenge be?

Furthermore, as noted so often, the two halves of the *Abba* Prayer are externally in synonymous parallelism with one another. But the first half, on God's name, kingdom, and will, was also internally a crescendo parallelism in which God's eternal will for the earth was the climax of God's name and God's kingdom. We therefore expect a similar crescendo parallelism in this second half, from bread through debts to temptation. In other words, the temptation clause must bring the second half to some sort of peak challenge. What, then, is that climactic vision?

Finally, as we prepare to answer that question in our final chapter, I draw attention to certain other guiding points for the discussion. One guiding point concerns format. The structure of the final challenge is a "not . . . but," synonymous parallelism of a negative and a positive sentence. This is the only example of that format in the entire prayer, and it puts the entire second half in a sequence of positive ("bread"), negative ("debt"), negative ("lead us not"), positive ("deliver us from"). We are, as seen so often before, praying a poetic hymn in which every word is in its proper place.

Another guiding point concerns content. I take very seriously that God is asked not to "*lead* us into temptation." Is it enough to say that, since God controls the earth, everything that happens, whether good or evil, comes from God? For example, the Bible says that, before the Exodus from Egypt, God "hardened the heart of Pharaoh," so that he refused to let Israel depart (Exod. 9:12; 10:1, 20, 27; 11:10; 14:8). Would that be but another way of saying that God "led him into temptation"?

Despite that, I still find the verb "lead" too strong as a simple admission of general divine control. I want to explore in the next chapter whether there is some more specific content to "do not *lead* us into temptation" as addressed to God. I also wonder whether we are imagining all temptations in some very general sense or whether some more specific one is intended.

8

Lead Us Not into Temptation

And lead us not into temptation, but deliver us from evil.

Matthew 6:13, KJV

And do not bring us to the time of trial, but rescue us from the evil one.

Matthew 6:13, NRSV

"Fortune, indeed, had from all quarters passed over to them," wrote Josephus of the Romans in his *Jewish War,* "and God, who went the round of the nations, bringing to each in turn the scepter of empire, now rested over Italy" (5.367). In 4 BCE, around the time Jesus was born, that imperial scepter rested heavily on Sepphoris, capital city of the Galilee, just a few miles north of Nazareth.

Herod the Great, "Friend of the Romans" and "King of the Jews," died in the spring of that year, and revolts broke out immediately all over the Jewish homeland. It was not a centrally controlled rebellion but involved bandit groups, disbanded soldiers, and even messianic pretenders in different regions of the country. A rebel named "Judas got together a large number of desperate men at Sepphoris in Galilee," according to Josephus in his *Jewish Antiquities,* "and there made an assault on the royal palace, and having seized all the arms that were stored there, he armed every single one of his men and made off with all the property that had been seized there" (17.271).

Rome's military strategy was to keep the legions on frontier duty guarding the great rivers to the north and the great deserts to the east and south around its protected Mediterranean core. There were no legions stationed at that time in Israel, but four were stationed just south of Antioch, capital of Rome's Syrian province, to protect the Euphrates frontier against the Parthian Empire.

Any southern deployment from those fixed Syrian camps opened Rome's eastern border to that imperial Parthian rival. When those legions marched against Israel, they marched with fire and sword. We will teach you a lesson, they said, and, if we have to return, it will not be for a couple of generations. Watch the dates: they came in 4 BCE, they came in 66 CE, and they came in 132 CE. They never had to come again.

In 4 BCE, the Syrian governor, Publius Quinctilius Varus, left only one legion in Jerusalem to quell those revolts. But very soon he had to lead two other legions to its aid. That meant twelve thousand more elite troops accompanied by two thousand auxiliary cavalry and fifteen hundred auxiliary infantry. He was also accompanied by "Aretas of Petra," from the Transjordanian Nabateans, "who, in his hatred of Herod, also sent a considerable force of infantry and cavalry" (*Jewish Antiquities* 17.287).

When Varus reached his staging area at Ptolemais on the Mediterranean coast near modern Haifa, he divided his command. He himself led the main force southward to Jerusalem, where "the number of those who were crucified on the charge of revolt was two thousand" (*Jewish Antiquities* 17.295). But, for my present purpose, Varus had first "turned over part of his army to his son and to one of his friends, and sent them out to fight against the Galileans who inhabit the region adjoining Ptolemais. His son attacked all who opposed him and routed them, and after capturing Sepphoris, he reduced its inhabitants to slavery and burnt the city" (17.288–89).

From the tiny hamlet of Nazareth you went first up over the ridge and then around ancient swamps on the valley floor four or five miles to reach the city of Sepphoris. Josephus does not tell us what happened to Nazareth when that legion destroyed nearby Sepphoris in 4 BCE. But we can easily imagine it from the account in his *Jewish War* of what happened to other small villages as the Roman legions and their Arab allies continued south toward Jerusalem:

> They encamped near a village called Arous [in Samaria, which was] sacked by the Arabs. Thence Varus advanced to Sappho [in Judea], another fortified village, which they likewise sacked, as well as the neighboring villages which they encountered on their march. The whole district became a scene of fire and blood and nothing was safe against the ravages of the Arabs. Emmaus, the inhabitants of which had fled, was burnt to the ground by the orders of Varus. (2.69–70)

That is what would have happened to Nazareth and to any of Sepphoris's adjacent villages in 4 BCE. Grain, produce, and livestock would have been taken, and farms, houses, and trees destroyed. Those unable to hide successfully would have been killed if male, raped if female, and enslaved if young.

———

In a review of one of my books, a fellow scholar said: "The model that seems always to have been in Crossan's mind when discussing Jesus is that of Ireland, his own country, which the British conquered and colonized, exploiting the indigenous population."[1] I freely admit that *I am unable not to see* certain parallels between the attempts of those two small battered peoples—Israel in the first century and Ireland in the nineteenth—to maintain dignity and identity against those great empires that attempted to control them.

Here is one such fundamental parallel. Both peoples resisted nonviolently as well as violently. Nonviolent resisters often died as unarmed martyrs. Violent resisters often won the first round against the local trip-wire troops, but massacre ensued when imperial reinforcements arrived. But, I insist once again, for both Israel and Ireland nonviolent and violent resistance were both in play. I knew that from Ireland, and it helped me to recognize it—but not to invent it—for Israel. I certainly look, therefore, at Jesus and his first-century Jewish context with Irish eyes unsmiling, and I do so in these three narrowing circles of context.

In the wider context, Jesus lived in the lull between two violent rebellions against imperial oppression in his Jewish homeland. The first one was under Augustus at the start of the Julio-Claudian imperial dynasty in 4 BCE. The second was under Nero at its dismal end in 66 CE.

In the narrower context, Jesus lived in the midst of a series of nonviolent reactions to Roman control. Those involved the census for taxation in 6 CE, the provocative actions of Pilate in 26 CE, and the attempt by Caligula to have his divine statue erected in Jerusalem's Temple in 40 CE.

In the narrowest context of all, we are back where this chapter started. Jesus was born around 4 BCE and grew up in Nazareth, a village that would have "survived" the legionary attack on its adjacent city, Sepphoris. The Roman Empire, with its military power, was not some distant quasi-mythical entity as Jesus grew up in Nazareth. I cannot imagine that Rome's legionary incursion was not the main topic of song and story, legend and interpretation among the villagers. That is, of course, beyond proof or disproof, but I would wager my sense of history on its accuracy.

I imagine that legionary attack as establishing a terribly clear date in reference to which all other events were labeled "before," "during," or "after" in a world that did not run by our ticking clocks and turning calendars. I imagine—that is to say, *I cannot not imagine*—those villagers speaking about the "Year of the Romans" and Jesus listening and learning.

I propose, therefore, that Jesus, growing up in the years after that military incursion around Nazareth in 4 BCE, would have heard over and over again about *the year the Romans came*. From all that talk, what did the young Jesus decide about God and Rome, homeland

and empire, rebellion and resistance, violence and nonviolence? Where was Israel's God on the day of Rome's revenge? Was the biblical and covenantal God of Israel violent or nonviolent?

———

In Chapter 5 I asked you to hear the word "sin" and see what *content* came exclusively, primarily, or just especially to your mind. If "sin" meant for you a list of "sins," what was your list and were there priorities within it? I now ask you to do the same with the word "temptation." When you hear it, what *content* comes immediately to mind? Do you think of it as applying to one particular type or degree of temptation or simply as a generic term for all and any of them?

Look once more at how the *Abba* Prayer concludes with this classic and climactic example of synonymous parallelism in negative/positive format:

| and | do not bring | us | to the time of trial |
| but | rescue | us | from the evil one |

Those two lines are mutually interpretive, so that *God both leads us into and rescues us from test/trial/temptation by the evil one.* But that still does not tell us the precise content of that test or trial or temptation (*peirasmos* in Greek). Is it general or specific?

My proposal for this chapter is that "temptation" in the Lord's Prayer has a very specific meaning, not just a general one. There are certainly multiple types and degrees of temptation all around us every day—political, economic, and religious, local, national, and international. Who could name them all? But my suggestion is that the "temptation" that climaxes the *Abba* Prayer is quite specific in intention, quite precise in content, and quite deeply embedded in the concrete historical situation of first-century Israel's confrontation with the Roman Empire.

That content presumes those just-mentioned options of nonviolent *or* violent resistance before, during, and after the life of Jesus. It specifically asks God not to "lead us into"—yes, *lead* us into—the temptation of violent resistance to Rome's violent domination. Instead, it asks God to *deliver us from* that evil action or that evil one. It is, in other words, about avoiding violence even or especially when undertaken to hallow God's name, to establish God's kingdom, and thereby to fulfill God's will "as in heaven so on earth."

I have three types of arguments in favor of that proposal. One type involves all those presuppositions just mentioned about *reading* a Jewish Jesus *with* Irish *eyes*. (There is, by the way, no alternative to *reading with a particular kind of eye* for anyone, anywhere, ever.)

Another type presumes that bread and debt were not just hopes for life in general, but also specific criticisms against Galilee's Romanization, Antipas's urbanization, and the lake's commercialization in the 20s of that dangerous first century in the land of Israel. So, maybe, if the bread and the debt are specific, so also is the temptation?

The last type is, of course, the most important. It is everything that follows in the rest of this chapter. What does "temptation" or "trial" or "test" involve in the biblical tradition and especially in the New Testament itself?

———

I begin my interpretation of "temptation" (Greek *peirasmos*) in the *Abba* Prayer of Jesus with the "test/trial/temptation" (*peirasmos*) of Jesus in the wilderness at the start of his public life. Here are those three temptations in summary outline:

Turning stones into bread in the wilderness	(1) Matthew 4:2–4	(1) Luke 4:2b–4
Descending from the pinnacle of the Temple	(2) Matthew 4:5–7	(3) Luke 4:9–12

| Gaining all the kingdoms of the world | (3) Matthew 4:8–10 | (2) Luke 4:5–8 |

You can see immediately that the order of the three temptations is different in Matthew and Luke.

There is, however, a general scholarly consensus that Matthew has kept the original order of their common source and that Luke has changed it. Why? Because, for Luke, everything in his gospel—from the infancy (2:21–38, 41–52) through the death (13:22; 17:11–19:28; 19:45–21:38) and on to the resurrection of Jesus climaxes in Jerusalem's Temple (24:52–53). And so also with his three temptations. So from here on I concentrate on Matthew's sequence, but with some input from Luke's content.

I wonder, by the way, if we Christians take those three temptations as seriously as we should. If we think of Jesus as the incarnation of God, do they represent not only what Jesus refuses to do, but what God does not do either? In any case, even granted that anthropomorphic or human-just-like-us language, it is precisely as "Son of *God*" that Jesus is tempted to do, but refuses to do, certain things.

Be that as it may, Mark—as distinct from Matthew and Luke—gives only this terse summary:

> A voice came from heaven, "You are my Son, the Beloved; with you I am well pleased." And the Spirit immediately drove him out into the wilderness. He was in the wilderness forty days, tempted by Satan; and he was with the wild beasts; and the angels waited on him. (1:11–13)

Both Matthew and Luke give full details about the three temptations, and they also connect the preceding baptismal proclamation by God much more closely with the temptations in the wilderness.

They both mention God's announcement of Jesus as "my Son, the Beloved" (Matt. 3:17; Luke 3:22), but then they begin two of the three temptations like this: "If you are the Son of God . . ." (Matt. 4:3, 6; Luke 4:3, 9). Those temptations are the formal and inaugural testing of Jesus as the Son of God, and his success under trial is rather pointedly contrasted with the failure of Israel (God's "firstborn son") when tested by God in the desert (Exod. 4:22).

Matthew opens his version like this: "Jesus was led up by the Spirit into the wilderness to be tempted by the devil" (4:1). Notice the sequence: he is "led *by* the Spirit—*to be* tempted—*by* the devil." It is God, as in the *Abba* Prayer, who brings Jesus to his time of trial. Luke, on the other hand, mutes that divine causality by saying, "Jesus, full of the Holy Spirit, returned from the Jordan and was led by the Spirit in the wilderness where for forty days he was tempted by the devil" (4:1–2a). There is no "to be" now linking "by the Spirit" and "by the devil." Luke also closes with this: "When the devil had finished every test, he departed from him until an opportune time" (4:13).

Also, during the three temptations Luke uses only "the devil" (4:2, 3, 5, 6, 9), but Matthew changes from "the tempter" (4:3) to "the devil" (4:5, 8, 11) and climaxes with "Satan" (4:10). For myself, I do not think of that figure as a transcendental spiritual individual, but rather as Temptation personified and presented anthropomorphically. But notice especially how, *in Matthew's sequence,* the three temptations progress from personal and individual through corporate and communal to structural and systemic temptation.

The *first temptation* begins with the tempter's challenge: "If you are the Son of God, command these stones to become loaves of bread" (Matt. 4:3). In this opening temptation no biblical citation is given by the tempter, but Jesus refuses it by quoting Deuteronomy 8:3: "It is written, 'One does not live by bread alone, but by every word that comes from the mouth of God'" (4:4). Miraculous power cannot be used for personal use—even for that seemingly appropriate task of creating some bread after a forty-day fast.

The *second temptation* follows from that first rebuttal. The tempter picks up the challenge of "every word that comes from the mouth of God" and so quotes this time from the biblical tradition:

The devil took him to the holy city and placed him on the pin-
nacle of the temple, saying to him, "If you are the Son of God,
throw yourself down; for it is written, 'He will command his
angels concerning you,' and 'On their hands they will bear you
up, so that you will not dash your foot against a stone.'" Jesus
said to him, "Again it is written, 'Do not put the Lord your God
to the test.'" (Matt. 4:5–7)

The tempter cites Psalm 91:11–12, and Jesus rebuts once again with
a citation from Deuteronomy—this time 6:16. Notice also that, although the first temptation was utterly private, concerning food for
Jesus all alone in the desert, this one involves a public display of miraculous power. It tempts God to protect Jesus while Jesus "proves"
his divine identity. And, of course, "test" is *peirasmos* in Greek.

That is a fascinating and profoundly biblical theme: we humans
are tested/tempted to tempt/test God. The classical example is during
the transit from Egyptian bondage to the promised land in Exodus
17—the chapter after the one with the manna/bread parable discussed
at the end of Chapter 6. In Exodus 16 the people had no food, complained, and received "bread from heaven." In Exodus 17 they have no
water—something even more important than food in the desert. They
"quarreled with Moses, and said, 'Give us water to drink.' Moses said
to them, 'Why do you quarrel with me? Why do you test the Lord?'"
(17:2; see also Deut. 6:16; 9:22; 33:8; Ps. 95:8).

In the biblical tradition, it is normal and acceptable for God to
test/tempt us, but abnormal and unacceptable for us to test/tempt
God. Why? Because our covenantal character and commitment can
change like the moon, but God's is as steady as the sun. Our integrity
fluctuates and so God must test/tempt it more or less regularly, but
for us to test/tempt God is to doubt—at least momentarily—God's
fidelity to God's own covenantal character.

The *third temptation* is—in the standard tradition of a classic folk-
lore story—the great climax and grand finale of the three trials or
temptations. This time the tempter does not begin with "If you are

the Son of God" as in those first two temptations. He now knows that Jesus *is* the Son of God and proceeds from that basis. Therefore, also, he does not bother quoting any biblical citation of a "word from the mouth of God," as in that second citation. Instead, he goes straight to the temptation. I cite it in both versions, as they help interpret each other:

> The devil took him to a very high mountain and showed him all the kingdoms of the world and their glory (*doxan*); and he said to him, "All these I will give you, if you will fall down and worship me." (Matt. 4:8–9)

> The devil led him up and showed him in an instant all the kingdoms of the world. And the devil said to him, "To you I will give all this power (*exousian*) and their glory (*doxan*); for it has been given over to me, and I give it to anyone I please. If you, then, will worship me, it will all be yours." (Luke 4:5–7)

In Matthew the tempter simply asserts his dominion over the "kingdoms of the world," but in Luke that is amplified by saying that those kingdoms have "been given over to me, and I give [them] to anyone I please."

That is an extraordinary claim, and we expect that Jesus will immediately reject it. We expect him to cite some counterscripture like this one: "The earth is the Lord's and all that is in it, the world, and those who live in it" (Ps. 24:1). We expect him to say that the earth does not belong to the tempter, but to God.

But Jesus never denies the tempter's claim. He implicitly accepts it. He implicitly concedes that the tempter can give him "all the kingdoms of the world" at the price of demonic worship. He simply refuses that worship with a citation of Deuteronomy 6:13: "It is written, 'Worship the Lord your God, and serve only him'" (Matt. 4:10; Luke 5:8). But why did Jesus not deny flatly any demonic control over the earth?

Notice that, actually, the tempter never speaks of "creation" or "the world" or "the earth," but of "all the kingdoms of the world" along with their "glory" (Matthew and Luke) and "power" (Luke). That is the violent world of civilization—as demonstrated, for example, by the twentieth century—rather than the nonviolent world of creation—as demonstrated, for example, by Genesis 1. The tempter does not own and cannot offer to anyone the "world that God so loved" (John 3:16), but only that world we are told "not to love," for it contains only "the desire of the flesh, the desire of the eyes, the pride in riches" (1 John 2:15–16).

This is all so very obvious. Of course, Jesus—and any of us— should worship and serve God rather than Satan. No matter what they actually do, most people would probably not admit to worshiping Satan. But that is name-calling rather than content naming. What, then, is the difference in precise content between worshiping God and worshiping Satan? *To obtain and possess the kingdoms of the world, with their power and glory, by violent injustice is to worship Satan. To obtain and possess the kingdom, the power, and the glory by nonviolent justice is to worship God.* They are, in other words, two ways of establishing our world and controlling our earth.

The last and climactic temptation for Jesus is to use violence in establishing the kingdom of God on earth and thereby to receive it as the kingdom of Satan. *And so also for us.* Recall what we saw in Chapter 5 about humanity's original sin as escalatory violence in Genesis 4? As God warned Cain, "Sin is lurking at the door; its desire is for you, but you must master it" (4:7). Jesus's climactic test/trial/temptation— and our permanent test/trial/temptation—is to establish the kingdom of God *by violence.* That would equate the eschatological and the imperial kingdoms. That would conflate divine and demonic power.

———

Compare, therefore, these translations of this last section of the *Abba* Prayer of Jesus from Matthew 6:13:

KJV:

| and | do not lead | us | into temptation (*eis peirasmon*) |
| but | deliver | us | from evil (*tou ponerou*). |

NRSV:

| and | do not bring | us | to the time of trial (*eis peirasmon*) |
| but | rescue | us | from the evil one (*tou ponerou*). |

What is at stake in those differences?

On the one hand, the KJV is better than the NRSV in the first part of that poetic parallelism. It is not a request to avoid the "trial" of violence *by others against us,* but a request to avoid the "temptation" to violence *by us against others.*

On the other hand, the NRSV is better than the KJV in the second part of the synonymous parallelism. It is not about rescue from general "evil," but about rescue from the specific "evil one," that is "Satan," a Hebrew word meaning "Adversary." The major temptation of God's Adversary is to lure us into the escalatory violence required to obtain the power and glory of all the kingdoms of the earth. But what if we did that "for God"? That is truly the last temptation. That is why Jesus did not say to God, "Do not let the devil lead us into temptation," but "Do not you yourself lead us into temptation." The last temptation concerns violence done for the name, kingdom, and will of God on this earth.

One final point concerning translations. The King James Version of the *Abba* Prayer concludes with this addition: "For thine is the kingdom, and the power, and the glory, for ever" (Matt. 6:13b). There is no great problem with adding that phrase into the biblical text from the prayer's liturgical practice. But, since that threesome of kingdom, power, and glory first appeared on the lips of Satan in the climactic final temptation of Jesus, we must always intentionally focus that "thine" on God as nonviolent rather than on Satan as violent. Nonviolent justice or violent injustice is the essential choice between God and Satan and their respective kingdoms.

That interpretation of *our temptation* as *our temptation to violence* is confirmed by a consideration of the *Abba* Prayer in the gospel of Mark. In Chapter 5, we saw that Mark places that *Abba* Prayer on the lips of Jesus in Gethsemane and mentions God's "will" there as well (14:36). In Chapter 7, we saw that, elsewhere, Mark also mentions that prayer's theme of divine and human forgiveness (11:25). I return now to Mark's account of the agony of Jesus in the Garden of Gethsemane and, as in the Lord's Prayer, the subject is "temptation" (*peirasmos*).

In Gethsemane, Peter, James, and John are with Jesus. But while Jesus is praying, "'Abba, Father, for you all things are possible; remove this cup from me; yet, not what I want, but what you want'" (14:36), those three disciples are fast asleep:

> He came and found them sleeping; and he said to Peter, "Simon, are you asleep? Could you not keep awake one hour? Keep awake and pray that you may not come into the time of trial (*eis peirasmon*); the spirit indeed is willing, but the flesh is weak." (14:37–38)

That *eis peirasmon* is the same Greek expression seen above in the *Abba* Prayer of Matthew and Luke. Here again the KJV has "into temptation," while the NRSV has "into the time of trial." What, once again, is at stake in that difference? What "temptation" would Peter have avoided by praying alongside Jesus that night?

Jesus had already told the disciples that they would all abandon him that same night (14:27), but Peter said to him, "Even though all become deserters, I will not." Jesus said to him, "Truly I tell you, this day, this very night, before the cock crows twice, you will deny me three times." But Peter said vehemently, "Even though I must die with you, I will not deny you" (14:29–31).

And, of course, Peter does deny Jesus thrice that very night (14:54, 66–72). So, staying awake and praying with Jesus would not have changed the fulfillment of that prophecy. But to what other "temptation" did Peter succumb that night? From what other "temptation" might prayer to God as *Abba* have protected Peter that night?

My answer focuses on a crucial scene during the arrest of Jesus later that same night. I look at all four gospel versions because the differences and developments are quite fascinating. As you read the various accounts, notice the focus on *sword(s)*. There is the *defensive sword* to protect Jesus. It is both used *for* Jesus and rejected *by* Jesus. There are also the *offensive swords* to arrest Jesus. It seems to me that there is a deliberate textual interplay between those two types of swords in order to raise this question: Can the sword be used to protect Jesus against the sword?

In Mark's account the defensive sword is used without any mention of its rejection, but those offensive swords are also present:

> One of those who stood near drew his *sword* and struck the slave of the high priest, cutting off his ear. Then Jesus said to them, "Have you come out with *swords* and clubs to arrest me as though I were a bandit?" (14:47–48)

In Matthew's account the defensive sword is used to protect Jesus, but is rejected by him. Once again, the offensive swords are also mentioned:

> Suddenly, one of those with Jesus put his hand on his *sword*, drew it, and struck the slave of the high priest, cutting off his ear. Then Jesus said to him, "Put your *sword* back into place; for all who take the *sword* will perish by the *sword*. . . . At that hour Jesus said to the crowds, "Have you come out with *swords* and clubs to arrest me as though I were a bandit?" (26:51–52, 55)

In Luke's account the use of the defensive sword is emphasized by the disciples' opening question about it to Jesus. Its rejection is also emphasized by Jesus's healing of the damage it does to the wounded servant:

> When those who were around him saw what was coming, they asked, "Lord, should we strike with the *sword*?" Then one of them struck the slave of the high priest and cut off his right ear. But Jesus said, "No more of this!" And he touched his ear and healed him. Then Jesus said to the chief priests, the officers of the temple police, and the elders who had come for him, "Have you come out with *swords* and clubs as if I were a bandit?" (22:49–52)

Finally, in John's account only the defensive sword is mentioned. No offensive swords are explicitly noted. The user of the defensive sword is now identified as Peter. The use is rejected by Jesus, but for a reason different from the one given earlier in Matthew:

> Then Simon Peter, who had a *sword,* drew it, struck the high priest's slave, and cut off his right ear. The slave's name was Malchus. Jesus said to Peter, "Put your *sword* back into its sheath. Am I not to drink the cup that the Father has given me?" (18:10–11)

You can judge the importance of that incident by the changes and adaptations across those four accounts. Notice these main ones:

Defensive sword used: In all four versions someone—"one of those who stood near" (Mark), "one of those with Jesus" (Matthew), "one of those around him" (Luke), or "Simon Peter" (John)—strikes the slave of the high priest and cuts off his (right) ear.

Defensive sword rejected: In three versions Jesus admonishes the striker: "Put your sword back into place; for all who take the

sword will perish by the sword" (Matthew); "'No more of this!'
And he touched his ear and healed him" (Luke); and "Put your
sword back into its sheath. Am I not to drink the cup that the
Father has given me?" (John).

Offensive swords mentioned: Also, in three versions Jesus asks the
same question verbatim: "Have you come out with swords and
clubs to arrest me as though I were a bandit?" (Mark, Matthew,
and Luke).

In all cases the general purpose is to raise this question: If opponents use violence to attack Jesus, should his disciples use violence to
defend him? The answer is quite clear. Even when opponents use the
sword to attack Jesus, the disciples must not use it to defend him. But
if not then, when? If not then, never! But that is the precise "temptation" to which Peter succumbed in Gethsemane. Had he been praying
rather than sleeping, he might not, as Jesus told him, have entered
"into temptation" (14:38). Especially if, like Jesus there, he had prayed
the *Abba* Prayer.

———

We have just seen what happened concerning the defensive sword
during the arrest of Jesus in Gethsemane in Luke 22:49–52. But what
about that earlier conversation about defensive swords—yes, plural—
during the Last Supper in Luke 22:35–38? Do those two units con-
tradict one another? How are they to be reconciled as coming from
the same author? Here is what Jesus said before they left for Gethsemane—divided into two sections:

He said to them, "When I sent you out without a purse, bag, or
sandals, did you lack anything?" They said, "No, not a thing."
He said to them, "But now, the one who has a purse must take
it, and likewise a bag. And the one who has no sword must sell
his cloak and buy one." (22:35–36)

"For I tell you, this scripture must be fulfilled in me, 'And he was counted among the lawless'; and indeed what is written about me is being fulfilled." They said, "Lord, look, here are two swords." He replied, "It is enough." (22:37–38)

That entire section is found only in Luke. Taken by itself and especially with that terminal translation of the Greek *hikanon estin* as "It is enough," Jesus seems to be saying that "two swords" are "enough" to defend him. That, by the way, would be rather naïve—if taken as literal approval of defensive violence in the situation of the arrest. But those "swords" before Gethsemane in 22:35–38 must be read along with the "swords" that follow almost immediately at Gethsemane in 22:49–51. In that overall context, what does Luke intend by this conversation at the end of the Supper?

Jesus refers back to an earlier incident with that opening comparison of "when" and "now" in 22:35. I begin by looking at that earlier event, but first in Mark before returning to it in Luke.

In Chapter 4 I mentioned briefly how Jesus told his companions to go out and do exactly what he himself was doing. They were to heal the sick, eat with those they healed, and announce the presence of God's kingdom in that reciprocity of spiritual and physical power, building peasant community from the bottom upward.

There is massive scholarly consensus that we have two independent versions of that crucial eschatological collaboration. One dates to the 50s CE and was used as a source by both Matthew and Luke. Since German scholarship discovered it and called it *die Quelle*, "the Source," we usually refer to it as Q for short. The other major source used by both Matthew and Luke is Mark itself, and that dates from the 70s CE. I focus on just one element—the traveler's staff—which changed significantly from Q in the 50s to Mark in the 70s.

In the Q version of their mission instructions, Jesus's companions are told: "Take no gold, or silver, or copper in your belts, no bag for your journey, or two tunics, or sandals, or a *staff*" (Matt. 10:9). But *no staff* means that they travel without that minimum defensive weapon against small-time thieves or even village dogs. They might as well have had a sign on their backs: "Available for mugging." Offensive violence might be wrong, but surely at least the minimal defensive counterviolence implicit in carrying a staff should be permitted.

In the Markan version from one to two decades later, we find Jesus changing his mind about that no-staff rule or, more accurately, having it changed for him. "He ordered them to take nothing for their journey *except a staff;* no bread, no bag, no money in their belts; but *to wear sandals* and not to put on two tunics" (6:8–9). The staff, you will notice, is not only permitted; it is moved from last place in the Q version to first place in the Markan one. Sandals are also permitted now, but my present focus is on that transition from "no staff" to "staff."

I interpret that change from Q to Mark as a concession to the reality of small-time violence. We are still in the villages of Galilee, and those who proclaim the kingdom's presence can carry at least a poor person's minimal defensive weapon. The no-staff command is changed to permission for a staff—both on the lips of Jesus.

Turn back, now, to that just cited two-part section in Luke 22:35–38. The general scholarly consensus is that the first part in 22:35–36 is a pre-Lukan unit. Jesus first recalls the time "when I sent you out without a purse, bag, or sandals." That refers back to that Q unit in Luke 4:10: "no purse, no bag, no sandals." But then he changes it: "Now, the one who has a purse must take it, and likewise a bag. And the one who has no sword must sell his cloak and buy one" (22:35–36).

Just as the tradition changed from no staff to staff for poorer Christians, so it changed from no sword to sword for better-off ones. In both cases it is the same transition, from allowing no weapons at all to allowing at least ones for defensive purposes. But Luke quotes this piece of pre-Lukan tradition in order to negate it. In other words, what is said in 22:35–36 is immediately denied by what follows it in 22:37–38.

The disciples accept the permission on defensive weapons and start to take inventory. They reassure Jesus that they have two swords among them. What is his reply—for Luke? The Greek phrase *hikanon estin* should not be translated approvingly or even ambiguously as "It is enough," but emphatically and disapprovingly as "Enough of that!" (which, by the way, is how the Greek phrase is translated in the recent monumental commentary on Luke's gospel by Father Joseph Fitzmyer, S.J.).[2] In other words, both the unit 22:35–38 at the Last Supper and the unit 22:49–51 in Gethsemane conclude with similar dismissive statements about even defensive violence from Jesus: "Enough of that!" (22:38) and "No more of this!" (22:51).

All of those assertions and especially those rather tortured contradictions indicate that injunctions from Jesus against even personal defensive weapons—whether staffs or swords—were just a bit too much for his followers to accept. Accordingly, in very human fashion, they both admitted them in one place and reversed them in another. But, whether by affirmation or negation, they confirm for us that Jesus not only demanded nonviolent resistance, but that he also wanted it manifested externally, visibly, and symbolically.

Finally, therefore, we can name "the last temptation" of the disciples in general and of their leader Peter in particular. It is defensive counter-violence. The disciples must continue in prayer—rather than in sleep—to avoid entering into that ultimate temptation. They must especially avoid being led into that temptation "by God," that is, for Christ. We can easily imagine—and maybe even agree with—their protests. Even if offensive violence is forbidden by Jesus, surely at least defensive counter-violence must be allowed? But Jesus's negation of that exception is shown most clearly in Gethsemane. No, it is not acceptable for the followers of Jesus to use defensive counter-violence even to defend Jesus himself.

———

Five connected themes are interwoven throughout this book's meditation on the *Abba* Prayer of Jesus. A first theme begins by translating the patriarchal name "father" as the more appropriate term "householder." It accordingly understands God the Father as God the Householder of the World. And as the human householder makes sure that *all* in the household have enough, so also does the divine Householder. That is the awesome simplicity behind the Bible's acclamation of God as a God of "justice and righteousness." It is only just and right that all who dwell together—in household or Household—have enough.

A second theme is that, at the dawn of creation in Genesis 1:26–27, the divine Householder created human beings as "images" of that divine character. We are to collaborate with God as appointed stewards of a world that we must maintain in justice and equality. "It is required of stewards," as Paul says, "that they be found trustworthy" (1 Cor. 4:2).

A third theme is that, for Christians, Jesus is the "Son" of the "Father," who is the divine Householder of the World. "Son" is another patriarchal term, but also a very specific one in a world of male primogeniture, where the firstborn son—or the only son—is the sole heir of the household. Jesus is the Heir of God, the divine Householder of the World.

A fourth element is that Christians are called to collaborate with Christ as Heir of God. That comes from the collaborative nature of the kingdom of God as *eschaton,* that is, from our necessary participation in the Great Divine Cleanup of the World. We cry out "Abba! Father!" to quote Paul once more, in ecstatic awareness that we are "heirs of God and joint heirs with Christ" (Rom. 8:15, 17).

A fifth and final theme is how all of that comes together in the *Abba* Prayer of Jesus. It is both a revolutionary manifesto and a hymn of hope not just for Christianity, but for all the world. Better, it is addressed from Christianity to all the world. Better still, it is from the heart of Judaism through the mouth of Christianity to the conscience of the earth.

In that *Abba* Prayer the hallowing of God's name means the coming of God's kingdom so that God's eternal will is accomplished "as in heaven so also *on earth.*" Think again of a two-sided coin: one side of the coin proclaims the divine name, divine kingdom, and divine will; the other side announces enough human food for today, no human debt for tomorrow, and the absence of human violence always. Think now, have you ever seen a one-sided coin?

EPILOGUE

The Strangest Book

Two questions—or maybe even objections—have probably occurred to you as you read through this book, this biblical meditation on the *Abba* Prayer of Jesus. They focus on the claim that God as the divine Householder of the world house is a God of nonviolent justice. The first question or objection concerns *nonviolence* and the second concerns *justice*. And those two terms stand or fall together.

First, even if God is—from one end of the *Christian* Bible to the other—a God of *nonviolent* distributive justice and restorative righteousness, is that biblical God not also—or even more so—a God of *violent* retributive justice and punitive righteousness? How is that to be—or is to be—reconciled?

Think, once again, for example, of that magnificent vision repeated verbatim in two eighth-century BCE prophets. God, the nations of the earth proclaim, "will teach us his ways that we may walk in his paths." To what end? So that we beat our "swords into plowshares" and our "spears into pruning hooks," so that "nation shall not lift up sword against nation, neither shall they learn war any more" (Isa. 2:2–4; Mic. 4:2–3). But, if you continue through the rest of those same chapters, that peaceful vision changes utterly. Isaiah speaks of the "terror of the Lord" (2:10, 19, 21) and of the Lord's "terrifying the earth" (2:19, 21), and Micah describes "many nations . . . gathered as sheaves to the threshing floor" (4:12) and "many peoples beaten in pieces" (4:13).

Worse still, that vision itself seems to have been known and repudiated by the later prophet Joel:

Proclaim this among the nations: Prepare war, stir up the warriors. Let all the soldiers draw near, let them come up. Beat your plowshares into swords, and your pruning hooks into spears; let the weakling say, "I am a warrior." (3:9–10)

Is, then, God's nonviolent peace to be established by violent war? Is the God of the biblical tradition violent, nonviolent, or both at the same time?

Furthermore, even if the incarnational or "first coming" of Jesus was certainly nonviolent, what about the violence of his apocalyptic "second coming"? Think, for example, of this sequence in the book of Revelation, in the Apocalypse that is our Christian Bible's last book. Its final image is quite magnificent. It is, once again, a rhapsodic vision of a transfigured earth:

See, the home of God is among mortals. He will dwell with them; they will be his peoples, and God himself will be with them; he will wipe every tear from their eyes. Death will be no more; mourning and crying and pain will be no more for the first things have passed away. (21:3–4)

But to get to that glorious consummation where God "makes all things new" (21:5), we have scenes like these:

The angel swung his sickle over the earth and gathered the vintage of the earth, and he threw it into the great wine press of the wrath of God. And the wine press was trodden outside the city, and blood flowed from the wine press, as high as a horse's bridle, for a distance of about two hundred miles. (14:19–20)

I saw an angel standing in the sun, and with a loud voice he
called to all the birds that fly in midheaven, "Come, gather for
the great supper of God, to eat the flesh of kings, the flesh of
captains, the flesh of the mighty, the flesh of horses and their
riders—flesh of all, free and slave, both small and great.". . .
And all the birds were gorged with their flesh. (19:17–18, 21)

We wade to that land of peace through a sea of war. Once again, does
God—and now Jesus as well—establish nonviolent peace by violent
slaughter?

Here, then, is the problem. If both those versions of God and Jesus
are in the Christian Bible—*and they certainly are*—how do we Christians decide between them? Or do we simply create a divine cocktail
of so many parts violence and so many parts nonviolence according to
theological taste?

First and above all else, one answer to that problem must be dis-
carded immediately. It is often said by Christians that the God of the
Old Testament was a God of anger, punishment, and vengeance, but
the God of the New Testament is one of love, justice, and peace. That
answer will only work as long as you do not actually read the Christian Bible. If and when you do, you will realize that the just mentioned book of Revelation is the most relentlessly violent book in the
canonical literature of any of the world's great religions.

Back, therefore, from libel and lie, to our problem. The nonviolent and violent visions of God march in tandem from start to finish
throughout the entire Christian Bible. The nonviolent and violent
visions of Jesus march in tandem from the beginning to the end of
the New Testament. What, then, do we Christians do with that dichotomy? My answer—which is utterly and traditionally obvious—is
given with a visual parable.

Constantinople's monastic Church of St. Savior in Chora is now
Istanbul's Kariye Museum. Its superb collection of mosaics and
frescoes was created at the start of the fourteenth century, when the

Latins were gone, the Byzantines were back, and the Muslims had not yet arrived.

Above the door from the outer narthex, or vestibule, to the inner one is an image of Christ *Pantocrator,* that is, the "All-Powerful One," so named even as the Byzantine emperor was called *Autocrator,* the "Self-Powerful One." Both would have been haloed, by the way, but Christ's halo is distinctively cruciform. Christ's right hand is lifted in the traditional teaching gesture of early Christianity, with two fingers upright—symbolizing the two natures of Christ—and three fingers circled below—symbolizing the three persons in the Trinity. Christ's left hand holds the closed Book of the Gospel and, once again, the fingers on that hand are separated into groups of two and three.

Straight ahead, above the door from the inner narthex to the naos, or church proper, is another image of a seated Christ Pantocrator. At the left, Theodor Metochites—then second only to the emperor in wealth and power—kneels to offer to Christ a model of the Chora church, which he had restored with those magnificent mosaics and frescoes. He would also, by the way, end his life as a destitute monk and be buried in the parecclesion, or burial chapel, of that same church. In the mosaic he looks upward to Christ, who, ignoring him, looks straight ahead in typical Pantocrator fashion. As in the first mosaic, the closed book is in Christ's left hand and the fingers of his right hand appear in the formal teaching gesture.

To your right, down the inner narthex, is a small dome. In its center is another image of Christ Pantocrator. As in those two preceding images, his inner garment is brown, his outer garment is blue, the closed book is in his left hand, and his right hand has fingers raised in the teaching gesture.

That set, traditional image of Christ Pantocrator is found throughout the churches—and down through the centuries—of eastern Christianity. But here is my point: *Christ is never reading that book.* That is confirmed, for example, as you pass under that mosaic of Metochites and continue into the naos itself.

Facing you to left on the wall underneath the great central dome is yet another image of Christ Pantocrator. This time he is standing— still in brown and blue—and this time his left hand holds the opened rather than the closed Book of the Gospel. *But he is still not reading it.* Instead, it is opened toward us and tells us in the Greek of Matthew 11:28: "Come to me, all you that are weary and are carrying heavy burdens, and I [will give you rest]." That, of course, is not the book, but the Christ speaking to us.

From all of that, I draw this conclusion. Christ never reads the book, because *Christ is the norm, the criterion, the purpose, and the meaning of the book.* The book points to Christ; Christ does not point to the book. We are not the People *of* the Book; we are the People *with* the Book. The Gospel of John does not say, "God so loved the world that he gave us" a *book* (3:16). The Revelation of John does not say that we are saved "by the *ink* of the Lamb" (12:11). For over a hundred years Christians have asked WWJD? (What Would Jesus Do?) and not WWBS? (What Would the Bible Say?). If Christ is the norm of the gospel, then he is also the norm of the New Testament, and of the entire Christian Bible. That, of course, is why we are called Christ-ians and not Bible-ians.

That, therefore, is my answer to this Epilogue's first question. Confronted, *as we are,* by tandem visions of both a nonviolent and a violent God throughout our Bible, we simply ask ourselves another question. *Is Christ the incarnation and revelation of a nonviolent or a violent God?* Since Jesus the Christ was clearly nonviolent (thank you at least for that correct judgment, Pilate), we Christians are called to believe in a nonviolent God.

In other words, the nonviolent incarnational Christ challenges and judges the violent apocalyptic Christ. Our Christian Bible, therefore, tells a most strange story. It is one whose meaning is in the middle, not the end, one whose climax is in the center, not the conclusion. That is, by the way, why we Christians count time down to the incarnation of Christ and then back up from it.

Unfortunately, then, our Christian Bible has itself succumbed to the great temptation of the evil one, namely, to make God violent and Jesus the revelation of that violent God. But the final and climactic unit of the *Abba* Prayer pleads against that desecration. It challenges us, first, to go back through our Bible and notice that other God, the God *not* of violent retributive justice and punitive righteousness, *but* of nonviolent distributive justice and restorative righteousness. And it challenges us, second, to think about Jesus as creator of the *Abba* Prayer and to ask ourselves: Do we find any divine violence in it? Or do we find in it—and in the life that produced it as its summary—a nonviolent vision that is still the last best hope for our species and our earth?

———

The second major question or objection concerns that word *justice* itself, even when it is taken to mean equitable distribution rather than stern retribution. In public lectures, when I avoid anthropomorphic language and speak of God as Justice rather than of God as just, I very often get the objection that God is not Justice, but Love. I am told—quite correctly—that nowhere in the Christian Bible does it say that "God is Justice," but it says twice in 1 John that "God is Love":

Whoever does not love does not know God, for *God is love.* (4:8)

So we have known and believe the love that God has for us. *God is love,* and those who abide in love abide in God, and God abides in them. (4:16)

Should divine justice and divine love be played off against each other and, if not, how are they to be reconciled in Christian consciousness?

Is it enough simply to combine them? Is it enough to note—quite correctly—that texts in the Christian Bible speak *both* of a God of justice in Isaiah 30:18 and Malachi 2:17 *and* of a God of love in 2 Corinthians 13:11? Is it enough to say—quite correctly—that "love" in the Bible is not just emotional but operational, not just about feeling but about acting? Is it enough to insist—quite correctly—that for John (e.g., 13:34) and Paul (e.g., Rom. 13:8) "loving one another" means "sharing" with one another? I think, however, that we must move toward a much closer correlation of justice and love than any of those suggestions.

On the one hand, so many individuals and groups who have started out with a dream of distributive justice for all peoples have ended up in bloody slaughter. One way to establish that justice would be to kill all those who oppose it. Why, in other words, does distributive justice tend so often to end up in violence?

On the other hand, "love," that most precious word in our language, refers to an almost unimaginable range of referents—from, say, our favorite candy bar to the soul mate of our life, from, say, our favorite sports team to God Almighty. If "justice" tends so often to go wrong, why does "love" tend so often to be empty? Could it be that love is a style or mode of justice, so that you can never have either alone?

We speak of a human being as composed of flesh and spirit or of body and soul. Combined, they form a human person; separated, what's left is a human corpse. When body and soul or flesh and spirit are separated, we do not get two persons; we get one corpse. Think, then, of justice as the body of love and love as the soul of justice. Think, then, of justice as the flesh of love, and love as the spirit of justice. Combined, you have both; separated, you have neither. Justice without love or love without justice is a moral corpse. That is why justice without love becomes brutal and love without justice become banal.

In the late 1940s I was in boarding high school at St. Eunan's College in Letterkenny, County Donegal, Ireland. When we studied poetry—Irish or British—we had to learn the poems by heart before discussing them. So, in my very early teens, I learned that in John Keats's "Ode on a Grecian Urn" this is the urn's message: "'Beauty is truth, truth beauty,'—that is all / Ye know on earth, and all ye need to know."

Now, almost sixty years later, I summarize what I have learned from this book's biblical meditation on the *Abba* Prayer of Jesus by imaging an alternative "Ode on a Biblical Urn." The urn is made not of ceramic, but of stone, and it tells us: "Justice is love, love is justice. That is all we know on earth, and all we need to know."

Appendix

Matthew 6:9–13	**Luke 11:2–4**	***The Teaching (Didachē)* 8.2**
Our Father in the heavens,	Father,	Our Father in heaven,
hallowed be your name.	hallowed be your name.	hallowed be your name.
Your kingdom come.	Your kingdom come.	Your kingdom come.
Your will be done, as in heaven so on earth.		Your will be done, as in heaven so on earth;
Give us our daily bread today	Give us our daily bread each day	Give us our daily bread today
And forgive us our debts,	And forgive us our sins,	And forgive us our debt
as we also have forgiven our debtors.	for we ourselves forgive everyone indebted to us.	as we forgive our debtors.
And lead us not into temptation,	And lead us not into temptation	And lead us not into temptation,
but deliver us from the evil one.		but deliver us from the evil one, for yours is the power and the glory for ever.

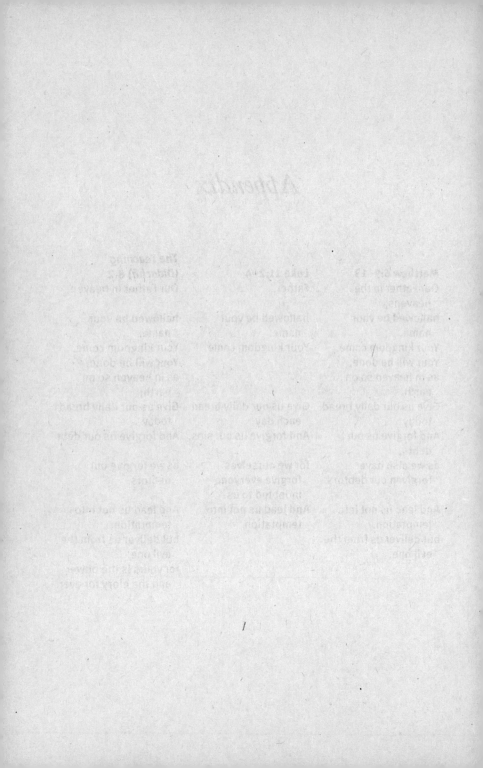

Notes

CHAPTER 2: OUR FATHER IN HEAVEN

1. Henry Rago, "The Promising," in *A Sky of Late Summer* (New York: Macmillan, 1963); "The Poet in His Poem," *Poetry*, March 1969.

CHAPTER 5: YOUR WILL BE DONE ON EARTH

1. Frederick Taylor, *Dresden: Tuesday, February 13, 1945* (New York: HarperCollins, 2004), p. 75.

CHAPTER 6: GIVE US OUR DAILY BREAD

1. Shelley Wachsmann, *The Sea of Galilee Boat: An Extraordinary 2000-Year-Old Discovery* (New York: Plenum, 1995), p. 358.
2. Wachsmann, *Sea of Galilee Boat*, p. 147.

CHAPTER 8: LEAD US NOT INTO TEMPTATION

1. E. P. Sanders, "Who Was Jesus?" a review of *Excavating Jesus*, by John Dominic Crossan and Jonathan L. Reed. *New York Review of Books*, April 10, 2003, p. 51.
2. Joseph Fitzmyer, S.J., *The Gospel According to Luke* (2 vols. with continuous pagination. AB 28–28a. Garden City, NJ: Doubleday, 1981–85), p. 1428.

Further Reading

Three excellent sources of further information are:

Davis, Ellen F. *Scripture, Culture, and Agriculture: An Agrarian Reading of the Bible.* New York: Cambridge University Press, 2009.

Lowery, Richard H. *Sabbath and Jubilee: Understanding Biblical Themes.* St. Louis, MO: Chalice Press, 2000.

Wright, Ronald. *A Short History of Progress.* The 2004 Massey Lectures. Co-sponsored by CBC Radio, House of Anansi Press, and Massey College at the University of Toronto. Toronto: Anansi Press, 2004.

Reading and Discussion Guide
for *The Greatest Prayer*

Prologue: The Strangest Prayer

1. Before you began *The Greatest Prayer,* what were your impressions of the Lord's Prayer? What did you think it was about?

2. Crossan reveals the poetic parallelism of the prayer. How does its literary structure change how you approach and interpret the prayer?

3. At the end of the prologue, Crossan states that this is not just Christianity's greatest prayer, but that it "speaks to all the world." How can a prayer by the central character of a particular religion be universal?

Chapter 1: Pray Then in This Way

1. Crossan maintains that the earliest form of the Lord's Prayer was simply the phrase "*Abba*, the Father." What does this simple phrase mean, as a prayer, to you? What if this was the entire prayer—would it be effective? Why or why not?

2. Do you agree that a "mature prayer life" means moving from request and gratitude to empowerment? How have you worked toward this in your own life?

3. Crossan states that this prayer and a commitment to distributive justice are inseparable—like two sides of a coin.

He argues that Jesus, like Paul, teaches that we are "heirs of God"—that is, we have a co-responsibility to help run God's world and make sure everyone/thing has enough. How does this outlook change how you view the world and your role in it? Is this responsibility empowering? Intimidating?

Chapter 2: Our Father in Heaven

1. If you pray the Lord's Prayer, has the male-dominated language tripped you up in the past? Why or why not? Does Crossan's explanation of the inclusive nature of the word "Father" help you?

2. Crossan says that the best way to think of what the biblical writers meant by "Our Father in Heaven" is as "Householder of the Earth"—he who takes care of the earth and everything on it. How does this change your conception of God? How does this change how you understand God's role in the world?

3. On page 49, Crossan says, "What happens to God and what happens to us are interactive, reciprocal, and collaborative." How do you feel about this? Is it presumptuous or empowering to say that God can't, or won't, effect change without us?

Chapter 3: Hallowed Be Your Name

1. Crossan argues that God is holy because he seeks justice for all. How does this change how we might "make holy" God's name?

Chapter 4: Your Kingdom Come

1. When you have prayed "Your kingdom come" in the past, what did you mean? Were you thinking God's kingdom here on earth, or a heavenly kingdom in the future? Does

Crossan's interpretation of how Jesus might have meant "kingdom" as a nonviolent, present, and collaborative state change the way in which you will pray these words?

2. Read again Desmond Tutu's quote on page 94: "God, without us, will not; as we, without God, cannot." What role, then, do humans play in God's work according to Tutu's prayer? Do you think God works collaboratively with us? How does this change our conception of how we live?

Chapter 5: Your Will Be Done on Earth

1. Crossan argues that what is wrong with the world (sin) is the natural "consequence" of injustice rather than a violation that needs to be atoned for in order to escape divine "punishment." Can you think of ways in which sin and its punishment work as "consequence"?

2. If God is not seen primarily as the judge and punisher of sin and more as the restorer of justice and harmony, how might this change how and where we see God being active in the world? What do you think you might be asking for when you pray for God's will to be done "on earth as it is in heaven"?

Chapter 6: Give Us Our Daily Bread

1. In chapter 6, Crossan argues that "daily bread" calls up all the bread and fish stories scattered throughout the gospels—the feeding of the five thousand, Jesus directing fishermen where to fish, the Last Supper—all emphasizing that God's plan is for a just distribution of food so that no one has to worry about hunger, today and including all tomorrows. How does this change where you look for answers when you pray "give us this day our daily bread"? What does "food" or "bread" symbolize for you? How do you connect God and "our daily bread"?

Chapter 7: Forgive Us Our Debts

1. The biblical notion of "debt" is tied closely to "slavery" and the hope of redemption and freedom. Crossan argues that Jesus's call for the forgiveness of "debts" should be taken literally. God's justice, as embodied in his redemption of Israel's enslavement in Egypt, calls for the forgiveness of our debts and our pledge to forgive the debts of others. When you imagine yourself free from all your debts, what comes to mind? Why is being forgiven our debts connected to forgiving the debts of others? What would it look like in your life to live by this prayer more fully?

Chapter 8: Lead Us Not into Temptation

1. Most people think of temptation as an immoral inclination to do an evil act. But Crossan argues that "temptation" has a precise meaning, in this context, of using violence—even if your goal is a good and noble one. In that light, how does this portion of the prayer change its meaning for you? Likewise, what does it mean for you to ask to be "rescued from the evil one"? What does a commitment to nonviolence mean to you?

Epilogue: The Strangest Book

1. How has your view of the Lord's Prayer changed after reading this book? How has it changed what you believe you are praying for when you recite these ancient words?

2. Crossan calls the Lord's Prayer "a hymn of hope" and a "revolutionary manifesto." What does each phrase mean to you? Do you agree with those descriptions? Why or why not?